Facing the Unfathomable

Surviving your son's suicide

CHRISTINE PEDLEY

© Christine Pedley 2024, All rights reserved

www.pedleywrites.au
Socials @christinepedley
First (eBook/paperback) edition: September 2024

The right of Christine Pedley to be identified as the author of this work has been asserted by her in accordance with Copyright Amendment (Moral Rights) Act 2000. All rights reserved. The author retains moral and legal rights. Apart from any use as permitted under Copyright Act 1968, no part of this publication may be reproduced, scanned, stored in a retrieval system, recorded or transmitted in any form of by any means, electronic, mechanical, photocopying, recording or otherwise, without prior permission of the author.

Some names and identifying details have been changed to protect the privacy of individuals. Any likeness to other persons either living or dead is purely coincidental.

This book is intended as general information only and should not be used to diagnose or treat any health condition. In light of the complex, individual, and specific nature of health problems, this book is not intended to replace professional medical advice.

The ideas, procedures, and suggestions in this book are intended to supplement, not replace, the advice of a trained medical professional. Consult your physician before adopting any of the suggestions in this book, as well as about any condition that may require diagnosis or medical attention. The author disclaims any liability arising directly or indirectly from the use of this book.

Design: WorkingType Book Design
Editor: Rebecca Wylie / Sage Written Word

 A catalogue record for this book is available from the National Library of Australia

www.trove.nla.gov.au

ISBN: 978-1-7636586-0-8 (pbk)
ISBN: 978-1-7636586-1-5 (ebook)

Jonathan Daniel Peck
You continue to inspire me
A life is complete when it comes to an end

Foreword

As a witness to just a fragment of the grief Christine has experienced after Jono died, reading this insightful recount of her depths of pain, sorrow, and the everyday journey she has and continues to walk is so heartfelt and clarifying.

This book may provide a lifeline in your own tumultuous sea of sorrow. It may serve as a guiding light for you as a parent grappling with the unimaginable death of your child. It may provide a sense of knowing and resilience, or it may simply provide valuable tools to assist you in knowing the right thing to say to a bereaved person.

This book intertwines Christine's wisdom from various disciplines, incorporating psychological insights and practical advice, and it creates a tapestry of understanding that speaks directly from the heart.

In the midst of sorrow, Christine's book emerges as a beacon of solace, reminding us of the power of love. It is like a gentle embrace, assuring us that our emotions are valid and that support surrounds us, even in the darkest of times.

Sue Williams

Holistic Mentor
Essential Healing Centre

Contents

Introduction	1
Chapter One: The event	6
Chapter Two: Returning home	13
Chapter Three: Who was Jono?	25
Chapter Four: The padlock of love	37
Chapter Five: The vigil and the funeral	55
Chapter Six: Walking the traumatic grief path	67
Chapter Seven: It's all in the timing	87
Chapter Eight: The golden rule	105
Chapter Nine: Putting the focus on theories	110
Chapter Ten: The power of language	125
Chapter Eleven: Gifts, support and a glimmer of hope	137
Chapter Twelve: Final thoughts and reflections	163
Support	182
A selection of resources	184
References	186
Acknowledgements	188
About The Author	190

Introduction

'Please make sure you're sitting down. I'm sorry to tell you that our youngest son is no longer on this earth.'

This was the phone call I received from my former husband while I was visiting my family in New Zealand. I had come to offer support to the families of three people who had died since my last trip.

He had rung to tell me my 31-year-old son had died that day by throwing himself in front of a train. The date was Thursday 2 June 2022. It was five days before Jono turned 32. He was a successful junior lawyer who had recently purchased his first home. Four days previously, I had shared afternoon tea with him. It was the day before I travelled to New Zealand.

This was my beautiful, beloved son.

Death wasn't new to me. I had been a social worker and I had worked in palliative care. The field of death, dying and grief had been my profession for many years. I was now a death doula and a funeral celebrant. I had spent many years learning about grief and gaining much knowledge in this area. At the moment of the phone call, all of my previous 'knowledge' felt like it belonged to a different world. There was no possible preparation.

Don't expect to find any normalcy, or even a 'new normal', after your child takes their own life because it won't happen. Normal ceases to exist. Emotions, thoughts and feelings that I had never experienced before took over what used to be my life. All my previous knowledge of death, dying and grief were replaced with a deep black hole that I did not recognise. I thought I had an understanding of the concept of suicide bereavement, and yet now I was faced with my own reality and it was nothing like I thought I knew. It was the most crushing pain I could ever imagine.

Nothing was the same again.

I no longer believe that all people who take their own life have a history of mental health, or that there is a predictability when someone is about to take their own life.

If you ask when I lost my son, I might reply, 'If I lost him, I will go find him. He died.'

'Working through' just about anything after the death of one's child feels impossible.

If you try to ask me how my 'grief process' is going, I immediately think of processed food, like ham from the deli.

And if you are like many other people and use the term 'committed suicide', then I shall gently explain why I find these words offensive. See chapter ten for more on this.

I refuse to let my grief be generalised or categorised. What happens to a parent when their child takes their own life is like a thumbprint: unique in every way. My experience of my son taking his own life is unique to me because I am who I am, and my son was who he was. His death, and my grief, while intertwined with the experience of others who face the same awful news, can never be duplicated. I am sure that if you have your own experience of your child dying you will understand how I feel. We are somehow connected to a group we would rather not be a part of, and yet our own individual experience is unique to each of us.

If you hope to read about professional and therapeutic responses for parents whose children take their lives, then you will not find it in this book. I am not writing from a 'professional' perspective. There are many other books that provide that, and I include some at the end of my book in the resources section. I do not subscribe to the notion that one has to have experienced bereavement in order to provide professional support, but I can say the personal experience of surviving the lived experience of your child's suicide offers a different perspective. As a social worker, I recall writing my own thesis more than twenty years ago titled *The Lived Experience of Grief.* Even then, I concluded that grief is an individual and personal response. If reading this book triggers some grief responses for you, please refer to the supports suggested at the back of this book.

What you will find in this book is a true, gut-wrenching account of how a parent has survived learning of their child taking their own life thus far, and an insight into the traumatic grief that follows. I will share with you some ideas and thoughts that eased my pain on some level, on some days.

The first part of this book takes you through the months following the death of my son Jono. The second part speaks to well-meaning support people and looks briefly at some grief theories. We finish on looking to the future and how to live with grief.

You will read about the seemingly endless tasks following a suicide.

You will read about an alternative way of planning a funeral, while considering the question, who is the funeral for anyway?

You will read my thoughts about grief and trauma feeling like a monster wanting to take parts of who I am, in small mouthfuls, and devour me ever so slowly.

One of the reasons I am writing this book is because more than 3000 Australians die by suicide every year.[1] I conservatively estimate that for every single person who dies, a minimum of six people are deeply affected.

Most people are not prepared for sudden and unexpected death. It is something that we don't truly learn about until we face it, and those lessons can feel awkward, confronting and uncomfortable. No one likes to feel all at sea. My hope is that this book may provide some insight and offer ideas for friends and family who are called to support the newly bereaved. It may assist with words and actions that are healing, rather than a response that feels awkward.

I also encourage professionals and counsellors to peek

inside this book too. Reading a lived experience may provide an additional perspective.

I have heard grief described as 'love with nowhere to go'. I challenge that and suggest that love is what will keep you going. Love from and to your child who is no longer on this earth, love from those beautiful friends and family you choose to surround yourself with, and most importantly, relearning how to love yourself.

Chapter One
The event

I love airports, especially when sitting at the gate preparing to board the plane. There's something magical in watching the flow of people coming and going, an air of excitement and anticipation. This day felt a little different though. There was a certain uneasiness, some kind of intuition within questioning if I should reconsider this trip to see my family in New Zealand. I tried hard to ignore it, as I had good reasons to travel.

My brother-in-law had recently died. His funeral had been held only two days prior. His wife, my sister, had died sixteen months before that. This was to be my first return to New Zealand since her death, and I knew things would be different. They had both lived great and long lives, well into their eighties. Being the youngest of a family of eight, I felt a new order had been formed. I wanted to support and provide comfort to my sister and my brother-in-law's adult children who had been through a lot in the previous couple of years.

I also wanted to be with my best friend. We had shared a friendship since our first day of primary school. Our lifetime friendship had seen many changes and different life events, such as marriages, children, career and study experiences,

Chapter One The event

divorces, re-partnering, and becoming grandparents. Now we shared the experience of death as her husband had also died the previous month. He had been my friend since I was fourteen, so I was sad that such a great person, who should have just been reaching the best time of his life, had died.

Having worked in the death, dying and grief field for the previous twenty years, I felt I had a reasonable understanding about the best ways to support those I loved, alongside acknowledging my own losses. I was always comfortable speaking about death in ways that honoured life, and I have always been accepting of the inevitable—that we will all die one day.

So, where did my concern for this trip come from? That part wasn't overtly clear. I did know that we were still living with the global pandemic, and I hoped that I wouldn't catch COVID-19, as I had not had it yet.

But the feeling I had … it was more than that.

The day before I left I received a phone call from my youngest son, Jono. He was 31 years old, and a successful junior lawyer at a top law firm in Melbourne. Just six months earlier, he had very excitedly purchased his first home. The phone call bothered me as he broke the news that a relationship was coming to an end. He described losing his capacity to trust his own trusting. He spoke of being totally bowled over. Jono was also in the middle of a very high-profile court case and felt he was no longer able to perform at his peak. We spoke at length as we discussed the unexpected bumps in life's journey and I had told him I would call him from New Zealand the next day. He was strong and he had a very large network of friends. Still, I was sad for him.

So, I sat at the gate, waiting to be called on to the plane, filled with an uncertainty but not fully understanding why.

Eighteen months previously, on my last trip to New Zealand, I had also experienced some hesitation about my trip. The reasons then had been obvious. We—me and my other Australian-based sister—were going back to New Zealand to say goodbye to our terminally ill sister. COVID-19 precautions were still in place so we were required to spend the first two weeks in a quarantine hotel. Quarantine had been an unknown and both my sister and I had been apprehensive and uncertain of the experience that was ahead.

This time, we were travelling from Melbourne to Wellington, and there would be no quarantine. Despite my concerns, we enjoyed the flight to Wellington and were looking forward to having another sister to welcome us at the airport. As I previously mentioned, I am the youngest of eight and I have six sisters and two brothers, the eldest sister now deceased.

Arriving in Wellington and feeling the warm, familiar hug from family felt reassuring. Things might not have been the same now that our eldest sister was no longer alive, but we all drew love and support from each other as we tried to accept and acknowledge our sadness.

We went directly to another sister and brother-in-law's home and enjoyed a lovely dinner while sharing some beautiful memories. We spoke about my brother-in-law's funeral two days before, including the large number of attendees. He had been quite specific about the hymns he wanted sung, and each of them had about five or six verses. There had been a lot of singing and no mask wearing. We all acknowledged that the world order had somehow changed with the eldest two members of our family no longer being a physical part of our gatherings.

After dinner, my sister who had met us at the airport took me to back to her home to stay for the first few nights, while my Melbourne-based sister remained with my sister and brother-in-law. We chatted more when we returned to her place before going off to bed. As promised, I phoned Jono to see how he was going. He talked about the challenge he felt returning to work the next day. I shared some strategies with him that I thought might make his first day back more manageable. We talked for around an hour and I just wished I had been able to give him a big mother hug, but I felt he would be fine after a good night's sleep.

The following morning began badly. My sister came into the kitchen, complaining how unwell she felt, and her throat sounded extremely sore as she spoke. I sent her straight back to bed, and after a COVID-19 test our worst fears were realised. Because she lived on her own, I felt pleased that at least I was there to look after her. The downside was that I was now classified as a close contact and had to remain there for the next five days. This was not quite what I had planned! By the end of that day, about ten more people who had attended my brother-in-law's funeral had been confirmed with COVID-19. Within two days there were about twenty or so people who had also tested positive. So much for singing without face masks!

When Jono and I spoke again that night, he was reasonably satisfied with his first day back at work. It had not been as bad as he thought, and he had managed to stay productive at the office the whole day. He still felt really conflicted about what lay ahead for him and whether the trip he had booked to visit his sister in the UK, to take place in two weeks, would still proceed. We discussed the benefits of spending time in London, and I suggested it could be just what the doctor ordered. He hesitatingly agreed and encouraged me to stay safe and do all I could to avoid catching COVID-19. I felt a sense of relief after the phone call as there seemed to be less sadness in his voice.

The next couple of days were spent caring for my sick sister while trying to keep my distance and stay as healthy as I could. I did not plan to spend my time in New Zealand sick with COVID-19, or any other virus. I had grieving family and friends I needed to support.

I briefly exchanged texts with Jono on Tuesday evening and I was pleased when he confirmed he was remaining positive and looking forward to spending time in London with his sister. My heart felt more settled, and when I heard nothing more on Wednesday evening I was happy that he hadn't needed to speak with me. I was comforted by the thought that he must be managing well with support from his many friends.

Chapter One The event

By the time Thursday arrived, I had endured enough of feeling cooped up and began counting the hours until my normal freedoms resumed. My sister had initially been quite unwell, but she appeared a little better that day, and she even got out of bed to eat dinner—in the other room from me, of course.

After clearing away the dinner dishes, I went to my bedroom for another night of reading and catching up on emails. I was getting closer to resuming my holiday plans, and it couldn't come soon enough.

My phone then rang.

I was surprised to see it was my former husband, Tony. We had been divorced for eighteen years, but we enjoyed a cordial relationship, especially when it came to our children. I was momentarily perplexed, as I couldn't remember telling him I was coming to New Zealand. I knew I had not given him my New Zealand phone number.

I answered with surprise in my voice, and the first thing he said was, 'Are you sitting down?'

I immediately felt a sense of panic from deep within.

'It's Jono, isn't it?' I asked, certainly not prepared for what was to follow.

'I'm afraid our son is no longer on this earth.'

I can only recall the low guttural screaming of the repeated word, 'NO! NO! NO!'

Even as I write these words, I can still feel the painful disbelief that echoed inside my head and within that bedroom.

It felt as though the louder I screamed, the more likely it was that I could make his words became untrue. Every fibre of my body wanted to scream and desperately fight against what he was saying. Those first moments of being told Jono had died were the worst moments I have ever lived.

My screaming brought my sister into my room, and for a moment we forgot COVID-19 as she listened to the rest of the telephone conversation. She gently placed her arm around me, offering me comfort as Tony shared what he knew. The police had only just left Tony's home. I was so glad his wife was with him.

Jono had jumped in front of a train late that morning.

Our son had killed himself.

The world had been turned upside down and I could not imagine how it would ever be able to be reversed. Jono was no longer alive. A dagger had just pierced my soul. I had no idea how I would continue to live in a world without my youngest son.

My beautiful, wonderful, clever, funny, much-loved Jono.

Chapter Two
Returning home

I was totally focussed on my urgency to travel home. I was hoping I could get a flight that night. I needed to be back in Melbourne as soon as I could—I just had to get home. I somehow believed if I was closer to Jono's body, I would be closer to his spirit. I needed to be with my immediate family. Perhaps if I got home quickly, we could somehow reverse this terrible mistake.

It was shockingly unbelievable. Jono had left home that morning to go to work, even sending some work emails during the morning, and then he had jumped in front of the train at 11:21 am. What had gone so horribly wrong?

I rang both sisters close by, and my Melbourne sister said she was coming to be with me. She was also in absolute shock. That dear sister was present when we welcomed Jono into the world, standing beside me when he was born. She had taken care of him during school holidays while I worked. She was his closest aunty. When I saw her, we stood in each other's arms and wept. There were no words. We wanted to reject the truth we were trying so desperately to understand.

I then had to ring my partner, Perry, to let him know what had happened. He was stunned and found it difficult to believe. He thought I was making it up. Oh, if only I was! I only spoke to him briefly because my focus was in trying to arrange my urgent return to Melbourne.

Because it was around 8:30 pm New Zealand time, it soon became obvious that there would be no flights available to Melbourne that day. Air New Zealand were not even sure if there were any seats to Melbourne the following day. I was desperate to return, and I felt powerless to get home quicker.

Shortly after that dispiriting conversation with the airline, my daughter from London phoned me. She and Jono had been inseparable growing up, and she had been his 'mini mum'. Despite an age gap of seven years, they had remained very close as adults. She was so excited for his visit and had been counting the days to his upcoming trip to London. Now there would be no reunion.

We could hardly translate our shock, our grief, our trauma into words. We were both just sobbing with unbelievable and incomprehensible jabbering. Our souls, our brains and our bodies were all trying desperately to comprehend something that was too unfathomable.

She and her two little girls were coming home to Australia, as quickly as she could. Jono had adored his nieces. Neither of us had any idea how we would make our journey home. We wondered how we could even manage to pack our suitcases. Small details, such as how we would get to the airport felt almost insurmountable. I didn't even know how I would be able to put one foot in front of the other. There were moments

I wasn't even sure if I was capable of even managing my next breath. But we both knew that we would soon be in each other's arms. We both knew we had to draw on an internal strength that was equivalent to the love we had for Jono.

My eldest son then called me, who, by this time, was now at Tony's home. The four of them—my son and his wife, and Tony and his wife—were helping each other to take one breath at a time.

When something is so inconceivable, there are moments when you really do believe someone will suddenly say, 'Oh there's been a mistake, Jono has just gone away for a couple of days.' But that did not happen.

The conversations from that night are a little blurry, but I do remember saying to my eldest son, 'Don't let anyone move Jono from the Coroner's Court. There is a particular funeral director I want to care for Jono and no one else is to touch him.'

Having been an independent funeral celebrant for the previous five years, I had become somewhat familiar with the funeral industry. I had a clear understanding of what I didn't want for Jono. Even in my state of shock, I felt strongly about making sure we gave him the best funeral. My preferred funeral director was one I felt would provide exactly that. I had never, in all my wildest dreams, thought I would ever be organising a funeral for one of my children. Apart from my own experience as a celebrant, I recalled the horror stories I had heard regarding some aspects of the funeral industry. The stories came from people who I offered support and comfort to during their bereavement. I did not want our family to be left with that sort of experience.

I have always been clear on my own funeral instructions and my children know them. After all, children arranging their parent's funeral is the order that should come naturally. What did not seem natural was parents arranging their own child's funeral.

Ironically, I was just a few days away from commencing training to become a funeral director myself. I strongly felt that this was my calling. In one sense, death was something I had become very familiar with. Before Jono died, I almost considered death my friend. I felt so comfortable entering a field that most others find quite confronting. If anyone was ready to work in the death field, I thought it was me. But not this death. What I experienced after being told of my son's death turned my understanding and familiarity of death on its head. I had no preparation for how to respond to the death of my child. It felt like a nightmare, and that none of this was true. His death had punctured my soul. Every cell and every atom in my body could not comprehend that Jono was dead, least of all how he had died. I felt so far away.

My three sisters, brother-in-law, and one of my beautiful nephews surrounded me with love in the hours that followed Tony's call. I was unsure how I should be feeling, or even what I should be doing. I had lived a very full life and I had always been actively involved with many things, and I felt confident

Chapter Two Returning home

in almost any situation.

What I was currently feeling was new.

It felt like I had entered uncertain waters with no navigational charts. That night, my body felt like jelly. I didn't recognise anything about myself. I was staring vacantly into a foreign chasm that had no ending and no direction. I had no idea how I would navigate the next few hours, let alone the rest of my life.

I was sipping a glass of wine when I received another phone call from my daughter. I could not remember what the wine tasted like—it felt like I no longer had capacity to judge or comprehend anything. I was being held in limbo, so uncertain of what the next moment might bring.

My daughter was trying to pack suitcases for her and her two children, still unable to grasp the reality of what had happened that day. We could not accept Jono's death as truth. All we knew was that we had to be together. My daughter's former husband was by her side, assisting with arrangements, and he was also accompanying them on the trip to Australia, bless him.

As I said before, Jono had been booked to travel to the UK to spend some long overdue time with his sister and much-loved nieces, which they had all been eagerly anticipating. The large gap of not seeing each other was due to COVID-19 lockdowns. They had even discussed by text, a day or two before his death, the places they might visit together. They had both been so excited to see each other again. The only connection my daughter now felt to him was the final text Jono had sent her.

I remember having a conversation with my brother-in-law that evening. Nothing about my life would remain as I knew it. I had difficulty imagining what the future would look like without Jono. Who would I become? Would I be an angry woman, or a depressed woman, or a freaky woman, or a bitter and twisted woman, or a total isolate? For a moment in time, it felt like I had disassociated from the world. I was looking at myself as a total stranger. I could not imagine what 'accepting' Jono's death would feel like, nor how it would shape me. If my spouse had died, I would become a widow, but what title do we give parents when their children die? Or would we rather not acknowledge it and somehow pretend if we don't talk about it, or give it a title, then life will still be 'normal'? A 'bereaved parent' comes nowhere close to describing the actual experience. Since Jono died, I have become aware of an alternate word describing who I am. The word is 'vilomah'. It comes from Sanskrit (a language dating back 4,000 years) and means 'against the natural order'. It is described as a powerful yet straightforward word that captures the pain and turmoil that a parent faces in this situation.

Such thoughts provided a distraction from facing the reality of my son's death. Even thinking or saying the words 'my son's death' did not make any sense whatsoever. It simply was not possible. The reality of my non-stop tears and crying was a constant reminder that something had happened. I had no map for this 'happening', but I knew it would change the rest of my life in ways I was yet to discover. I was treading brand new territory and nothing felt safe.

Later that night, I lay in bed, sobbing, unable to calm my mind. I instinctively knew I should try to get some sleep, but it did not come. My thoughts of Jono kept the tears coming and sleep became my enemy. I felt like I needed to stay in touch with what my body was saying to me, and I was afraid if I slept I may not remain closely connected.

Eventually, I think around five am, I did manage some very fitful sleep for a short period of time. When I woke, I showered and tried to think up a plan of what needed to be done that day, but it felt like someone had paralysed my brain. No idea or thought seemed able to connect to the next idea or thought. It almost felt like someone needed to lift my arm for me to clean my teeth. My brain had semi-frozen and no longer wanted to listen to my instructions. Only part of me was present and functioning. I knew how important it was for that small functioning part to keep going. Despite wanting to curl into a small ball in the corner of the room, my motivation to keep going was to be back in Melbourne with my immediate family. Every difficult moment was one moment closer to my return.

There were more phone calls to be made that morning. I called my New Zealand best friend, explaining to her the best I could that I would no longer be able to support her in her own grief because I was going home. She had no words either, other than absolute disbelief. I then needed to call a couple of close friends back in Melbourne to let them know I was on my way back. Each person I spoke with was totally stunned to receive the news of Jono's death. From the depths of my heart, I knew it would be my close friends and family who would be there for me when I felt I couldn't be. I knew it would be those people who would hold me when I couldn't stand, who would put their arms around me and sob with me, who would be there beside me to make sure I was able to keep going.

Needing to feel a connection with home meant I was almost in constant conversation with my eldest son in Melbourne. He and his wife were my strength and support during this time. I also spoke to my daughter frequently during preparations for her trip. Somehow, we tried to soothe each other, but neither of us knew how we could. I spoke again with Perry, my wonderful partner, realising just how desperately I wanted to be in his arms. He was also in shock, and he needed me as I needed him.

There was a moment that morning, as I sat on the edge of the bed with my sister's arm around me, when I felt something unrecognisable slowly arising from deep within. The 'feeling' translated into a deep wail. It was one I hardly recognised as a human sound, but I now understand it was my genuine **cry of grief.** It felt like my soul was being seen publicly by my expression. I continued to sob, loudly, without restraint, as my sister held me gently in her arms. My connection with another warm soul needed no words. Instead, it gave me just what I needed.

Chapter Two Returning home

That morning, I received a message saying something like, 'Hi Mum, I dropped my phone in the sink last night, and this is a temporary number I'm using for the moment'.

I was totally unaware of a phone scam that had been circulating and rushed to my sisters, questioning whether they thought Jono had sent this before he died. It had only come through that day, and I was totally confused, and even more upset. When I spoke to my eldest son, he told me it was a scam and to report it. What a preposterous thing to happen just hours after my youngest son had died! It almost dissolved me.

Finally, the news came that I was on a flight back to Melbourne later that day. I would be home with my family soon. I do not recall which family member arranged it, or how many hoops they had to jump through to get it done, but I suspect my beautiful nephew and one of my sisters had succeeded in what I had been told the previous day was impossible.

I was going to be home in Melbourne that evening.

My nephew's partner generously offered to drive me to the airport. I only have snippets of memory of that trip. It felt like every facet of New Zealand was brutally sending me on my way and telling me not to come back. Every building and every landmark were giving me a clear message which was 'just get out of here!'.

As we travelled beside the sea, there was a fleeting moment when I noticed a rainbow appear just above the water, but it was gone within a moment. Was that a sign from Jono? Was he trying to somehow make this trip easier for me? I like to believe so.

Sitting at the airport, waiting to board my plane, my eyes were drawn to families who had a son or two. I wanted to run to them and say, 'Hug your son, tell him you love him. Enjoy every moment because you don't know when it will be the last time'. Instead, I looked longingly at them.

It did not seem so very long ago that we made a family trip to New Zealand when Jono was an excited four-year-old. We were in this very airport. As a child he had devoured new adventures, but he always made sure I was close by. I knew then, as he grew older, his curiosity would take him around the world. I deeply yearned for that moment when he was a four-year-old.

During the walk to the boarding gate, my nephew's partner told me they had arranged for Air New Zealand staff to provide special support with my flights. To return home, I first had to fly to Auckland and then transfer to the international airport for my Melbourne flight. My sister who had travelled to New Zealand with me now had COVID-19, so she was unable to return to Australia just yet. Even though I was a seasoned traveller, having travelled solo across many countries in the world, I couldn't imagine how I would have managed this trip without someone beside me offering guidance and support.

When we reached the gate, my nephew's partner lovingly surprised me again by placing a *pounamu* around my neck.

Chapter Two Returning home

This is also known as New Zealand jade. It had been beautifully carved by my nephew and blessed by his family. In his words it was 'a gift from the mother (sea), beautifully complex yet reassuringly real and simple'. It meant I was not travelling alone. I haven't removed that pounamu from my neck since the day it was placed there.

The airline staff were nothing short of amazing in their care, consideration, and support of me throughout my entire trip home. It was dark when I boarded my last flight, and as I sat by the window, I felt strangely comforted by the new moon that stayed at my window the whole trip home. Looking at the moon somehow connected me to Jono's energy. Most of that trip was a blur. Most of the trip I cried.

As I reflect now, I can see how love was always carrying me. Even if I was not fully aware or able to acknowledge it at the time. Despite thinking I could not take another step, I had made it to this point. I knew it was because of love. The love my family had bestowed upon me had sustained me to this point. I also wondered if a portion of the love I was feeling may have come from Jono. Was that even possible? Some part of me wanted to stay in the sky forever. If I never landed on earth again, then perhaps I would never need to face the reality of Jono's death. Perhaps I could choose to stay in 'limbo' for the rest of my life.

However, I did land, and I was accompanied by another incredible airline staff member straight into the arms of my family waiting for me at Melbourne. There was my eldest son,

Tony, and Perry, my beautiful, supportive partner.

I was home.

I was in the same country where Jono's body lay. I now had to face the task of learning how a parent manages the grief and trauma when a son takes his own life. I was about to learn how to arrange a funeral for my child—a task no parent should ever have to do.

Chapter Three
Who was Jono?

I cannot talk about Jono's death without describing his life.

I have read so many sad stories from other parents whose children took their own lives and I feel deep compassion for them. I do understand the stories of relief when finally, their child is at peace after battling their mental illness for such a long time … but this is not my experience. Jono did not have a mental health issue. He was well loved and did not have any addictions or any mental health record. I believe the decision to end his life was not premeditated.

Jono died a very successful junior lawyer, working for a top Melbourne law firm. He had many friendship groups and was often the main organiser of them. I remember, not many years ago, when he and another friend initiated a book club. He was really excited about it, and even asked if I wanted to join in. I enthusiastically said yes, but after some thought, I realised it may inhibit him having his mum present. The book club continued to be very successful, with Jono being referred to by his friends as the linchpin. He was also well known for the very successful house parties he would have at his place.

Many of his friends told me how he was so good at connecting people, making sure all his friends knew each other.

So please, don't ever tell me that it is only people who have a known mental health condition or an addiction that spirals out of control who kill themselves. Don't tell me that people close to them usually know when their children are unwell or about to make wrong decisions. I don't want to hear the stories of parents' relief when finally, their child is at peace because their child had battled with living for such a long time. I will try to understand and feel the pain of parents who experience this, but it is not my experience. To the world, Jono appeared resilient and confident, which was even more shocking for his friends and family when he made that final rash decision.

My Jono should not have died.

Let me tell you more about him.

In 1990 we welcomed our beautiful 'surprise' package into our family. I had been working as a Young Women's Worker for a local council while studying for my Associate Diploma of Welfare Studies. In the middle of my studies, we discovered, much to our surprise, that we were going to welcome our third child into the family.

Tony has Nigerian/English heritage, and our daughter has similar features to her dad. She was always greatly admired for her headful of wonderful tight dark curls and her beautiful, tanned complexion. She was very excited at the prospect of welcoming a sister, and at six years old expressed great disappointment when I told her she was going to have a baby brother. She already had a 15-year-old older brother, and loved him deeply, but she longed for a sister. Instead of focussing on the gender of our unborn baby, I shared my anticipation with her of welcoming another little baby with the same beautiful skin and hair as hers, hoping that it might compensate for our new baby being a brother. But Jono was always full of surprises. He was born with a beautiful white English complexion, big blue eyes, and whisps of dark blonde hair! I then took a crash course in recessive genes to discover this was not an unusual occurrence for children with a rich heritage. Once my daughter held him for the first time, neither his gender nor his appearance held any significance for her. This was an immediate love story and from that moment she became his 'mini mum'.

We moved from one side of Melbourne to the other when Jono was around eighteen months old. Our family settled into life in Dandenong North, and he was a very much-loved youngest child and baby brother.

I continued with my studies and after our move, I took a new job as a housing support worker. Jono commenced childcare soon after. Somehow, he always appeared to be the favourite at the childcare centre. Perhaps I was a little biased, but it felt like he received premium care and love from each of the childcare staff. There were many occasions in the months that followed when the childcare workers were invited to our home for a meal or just visits. They seemed to adore him.

He started primary school as a happy if somewhat timid

child, but he was keen to learn about anything and everything. He remained at the same school, becoming school vice-captain in his Grade 6 year. Toward the end of his primary school years, his teacher would tell me she thought he was just asking questions for the sake of it. I was told that he would often try to 'argue' with his teachers about certain aspects of their knowledge. What they did not realise was that Jono had an insatiably curious mind. He would progress in his secondary school years to become a great debater. Naturally, this style of conversation extended within the family as well. I learnt very early on in Jono's life that he could somehow convince me that a black page was grey, simply by his persuasive and analytical style of conversation.

He discovered soccer around the age of seven and it remained his love for the remainder of his life. In fact, as a child, he would tell me that one day he would play soccer for his much-loved football club, Arsenal. He was good at soccer, but unfortunately he was not good enough for that dream to ever be realised. I spent many evenings sitting in my car, usually reading, or writing, during his years of training sessions. Our weekends were always planned around where and when Jono's games were. I learnt to love the sport too, but much to Jono's horror I continually struggled with the offside rule.

One of his many other loves in life was music. The enjoyment of both listening and making music continued throughout his life. The year I was completing my Honours degree in Social Work, Tony thought it was a good idea to purchase a drum kit for Jono. We lived in a small home and

Chapter Three Who was Jono?

there was one door between the drum kit and my computer/study area! It probably goes without saying that there were moments when I regretted the decision to introduce him to the drums. Despite any hesitations I had, he just loved it. He was a very successful drummer and passed grade one, two and three ANZCA exams with credit and honours, as well as playing in the school band and jamming with friends.

Jono was twelve, in his last year of primary school, when I separated from Tony.

He was deeply upset about this and for the first time ever, I saw him struggling with his emotions. People on the outside looking in never anticipated the separation between Tony and me. Nor had Jono ever expected this to happen in his family. I was determined to support and love him through this time and help him in the best possible way to feel less aggrieved by the situation. I felt Jono had the stamina to recover from this and to continue his journey into his teenage years without too much disruption.

It appeared to all, including myself, that this is what he did. He got through this adversity and focussed on his future. He had several friends whose parents had separated, and as Jono's parents, Tony and I tried to continue our ongoing involvement with him in all his activities. I know there were still moments he was sad that Tony and I were not living together, but his normal day-to-day childhood life seemed unaffected.

He was successfully accepted into the accelerated learning program at the local secondary school the following year and he soon adapted to being the small fish in a big sea, rather than the big fish in a small sea. He was keen to learn as much as he could, but he became quite frustrated with those around him who didn't share his passion for learning. He couldn't understand why someone would be down the back of the school graffitiing when they could have put that skill to good use in the art room.

He certainly was no 'goody two shoes'. A story was shared at his funeral by a friend from his class about the day Jono threw a piece of chalk into the ceiling fan, only for their work to be spattered with chalk dust!

He was very good at expressing himself through writing and I have a beautiful collection of poems, cards and letters he wrote over many years.

For my birthday one year, he gifted me a canvas that he had painted of the Chinese symbols for the words peace, love and happiness. This was beautiful on its own, but he also attached a beautiful note which melted my heart. It read:

On this day of mirth
We are celebrating the day of your birth,
'Tis a day worthy of great festivities,
But you might have to settle with lunch and a few pressies.

And what will you receive from your youngest son, you ask?
Some choccies and a wine flask?
No, unfortunately not, my dear mummy,

Chapter Three Who was Jono?

What I give you will not fill your tummy.
What it will do, though, hopefully, is just make you feel more at ease
And bring you hope, love and peace.
That is what I wish unto you my fun,
Lovely, resilient, super cool and beautiful Mum.
Avee amour, Jono

I recall a time discussing what the world might be like when he turned fifty. Without sounding morbid, I stated what I thought to be obvious, 'You do realise I may not still be alive when this happens?' I had been in my 35th year when he was born and quite logically thought that no one can guarantee being alive at 85. He thought about it for a while and came back to me with a little piece of paper he had torn from a larger piece, and it simply said:

To Mummy
Admit 1
To Sir Jono Peck's
50th birthday.

Somehow, in his mind, he thought if I already had the invitation then it would be rude not to stay around for the party. I found this little torn piece of paper after he died and still have it pinned to my notice board.

The day after his sister's 21st birthday party, he, along with 3,000 other boys, attended the Exhibition Building in

Carlton to sit the entrance exam for the prestigious Melbourne High School. He was delighted at his success and joined the Melbourne High School population in 2005, commencing at the Year 9 level. He really came into his own during the next four years. He successfully participated in things he had never tried before, including excelling at debating (which was no surprise to us, his family) and lacrosse. He loved learning anything new and remained passionate and enthusiastic about life. He would walk the corridors of Melbourne High with me, showing me the photos of very successful past students. He told me, 'One day my photo will be there too.'

His world of volunteering began while attending Melbourne High. The school program offered opportunities for students to volunteer their time at various places. Jono chose to be a volunteer visitor at an aged care facility. He enjoyed conversations with older people and would enthusiastically recall to me the life adventures of some of the residents.

He grew into a well-balanced young man and his curious mind proved valuable in him reaching high grades throughout these formative school years. He was focussed on his future career, but he still had the capacity to enjoy some fun times with his classmates and other friends. He certainly appeared to be driven to succeed. I remember on many occasions reminding him that I would be so proud of him no matter what he chose for a career. I was so proud of the young adult he was growing into.

Several months before the final Year 12 exams, Jono got very sick. I came home from work to find him in bed with a very high temperature and him telling me that he thought he was hallucinating. After taking his temperature and finding it was about 40 degrees, I rang for an ambulance. When the paramedics arrived, and I was out of the room, they asked Jono if he had taken any drugs. His answer was no, but he was really upset because he felt his integrity was being questioned. Once he arrived at hospital and was admitted, it was confirmed he had contracted meningitis. He was very sick for a few days, and I spent the first three nights sleeping beside him in a hospital chair.

He had several concerns during his time in hospital. The first was, as vice-captain for his school house, he was afraid he would let his team down if he didn't compete in the long-distance run that was coming up soon. The second was his concern about the impending end of year exams. He had been told by the doctors that he may experience some fatigue for some time once he was discharged from hospital. He felt his opportunities for a future university place may be in jeopardy, so we sought special consideration from his doctor to be used for his Year 12 exams.

The first concern was not warranted, as somehow he did manage to compete in the long-distance run (determination was a fine attribute Jono had), and he did not let his school house down. The second concern was also dismissed after he sat one of his 'practice exams' with a result of 98 percent. We did not submit the special consideration for his final exams.

He was notified from the Victorian Tertiary Admissions Centre on 15 December 2008 that he had achieved an ENTER score of 98.20. Although he was pleased, he wished it had been slightly higher! I was a mother ecstatic with happiness and pride. All his hard work had been realised and he was offered a place at Monash University for a double degree—a Bachelor of Arts (BA) alongside the Bachelor of Laws (LLB).

The next seven years at university provided him with more valuable opportunities. Jono seemed to have an insatiable appetite for all that life could offer. A standout example of this would have to be the many months he spent studying at a sister university to Monash in Prato, a city in Italy, not far from Florence.

He enjoyed living in Florence with friends, who were other law students from Monash University. When I visited him in Italy in 2011, we celebrated his 21st birthday at an exquisite Italian café. These friends gave Jono a great gift for his birthday, and I shared the benefits. It was a cooking class with an Italian chef! What a fabulous time we had, and I can say with honesty, despite never having done it before, Jono was the best 'flipper of crepes' on that night. When the cooking was done, we all gathered to share the meal, accompanied with some rather special wine. This memory, alongside many others, will be with me forever.

While he was at university, Jono continued volunteering his time for many organisations. It felt like he was born with a strong sense of social justice and he became an advocate for those who were disadvantaged or marginalised. He also described himself as a feminist. I loved watching him browse through my bookshelves and borrowing a selection of my feminist readings.

He met his first real girlfriend in 2012. They were both university students and met through mutual friends. He did tell me that the only reason I had met her was because he still lived with me at home. Despite this, I could tell he was quite smitten by her, and it wasn't long before they were considered a couple and shared many good times together. She was welcomed into our extended family and shared many happy family gatherings with us.

Five years later in 2017, Jono was admitted into the Supreme Court. As a family, we shared in his celebration that day, and when we all went to lunch together at a city restaurant the feeling of pride within me was enormous. My son had set his sights high and this was his achievement day. It felt like an abundant future lay ahead for him.

He was now enjoying his work as a lawyer for the same law firm he had worked for as a paralegal. He was always fully focussed on his career. Despite how busy he became, he still managed to fit in time with his family and close friends. We all shared a collective enthusiasm for his future.

In 2020, Jono applied for a judge's associate position in the Federal Court and was really pleased when he was accepted. This was a very intense time for him as he navigated his way around judiciary practices. Of course, he excelled at it and at his funeral the judge he worked for told me that Jono had been the best associate he had ever had.

In November 2021, Jono was involved in purchasing his first home. This was an exciting time, even if Jono felt a little stressed by all the negotiations with the bank. He said sometimes that he felt these negotiations had robbed him of a full workday, meaning he then had to spend many long hours in the evening completing his 'other' work, catching up on his daily life as a lawyer. He was no stranger to burning the candle at both ends, and he managed to somehow get by with little sleep on many occasions.

On the outside, life appeared to be going well for Jono. He was very committed to a class action case he was working on. I know there were times he felt under pressure, but he assured me he loved it and was managing the demanding work well. He was very enthusiastic and passionate about how the case was proceeding, convinced they would win.

Mother's Day on 8 May 2022 was really lovely. Jono had invited Perry and I, along with his older brother and sister-in-law, to his new home where he cooked dinner for us all. It was so lovely being together as family, enjoying his new home and celebrating the wonderful gourmet cook he had become. I loved that we were both enthusiastic in sharing recipes with each other.

It was only two weeks after the memorable Mother's Day dinner that Jono shared with me his sadness that comes when relationships and other pressures impact daily living.

On Thursday 2 June 2022, at 11:21am, Jono dove onto the tracks of an oncoming train and died.

Chapter Four
The padlock of love

When my daughter walked through those airport doors and into my sobbing arms, I knew we were at last all gathered ... but we were minus one. This was not how our reunion post COVID-19 lockdowns was meant to be. Jono had his trip planned for two weeks' time, and I had my tickets confirmed for an August holiday in London. It was supposed to be a joyous time filled with laughter and celebration, but instead our hearts were shattered. Instead of celebrating our reunion, we were planning Jono's funeral.

I lost count of how many makeshift beds we made up. We all stayed together for the many days that followed. Our home suddenly became the receptacle of all of Jono's love, filled with many tears and ongoing hugs amidst the confusion and trauma. There were moments when in comforting each other, we would find ourselves in a circle with our arms around each other. This became known as our padlock of love.

Our family received the generosity of so many people, demonstrated by the flowers, food and many visitors that showed up at my door. I was overwhelmed with the number of people responding to Jono's death. There were even those who had never met him but had heard about him through me or other members of the family.

I'm not sure how the following week would have been possible had it not been for my loving and caring daughter-in-law, along with my adult granddaughter, who both took responsibility for the running of the kitchen, including meal preparations. My brain was hardly able to take on the task of boiling the kettle, let alone planning meals for us all. It felt like there was a part of me that continued to feel partially paralysed. I could not decide if it was my heart or my brain that was refusing to function properly, or perhaps a little of both. I will always have so much gratitude in my heart for all those who helped with the practical day-to-day tasks that still needed to happen.

Tony and I, along with my son and my daughter, needed to attend the Coroner's Court to identify and sign the release of Jono into the care of the funeral directors. Reading that sentence makes it sound like a straightforward task that required attending to. Potentially, it was going to be a quick trip into the city and home again. I have difficulty in describing how I managed both the physical and emotional tasks of that day.

Meeting for coffee before visiting the court was intended to be an opportunity to gather our thoughts and calm us; however, calmness only very briefly visited that day. It felt like I was in a dimension of life that was not real and that everyone was just acting a role within a life drama. I imagined

Chapter Four   The padlock of love

we would soon return to how the world used to be, how it should be, with Jono still in it.

That did not happen.

As we walked away from the coffee shop, I read from the blackboard outside:

Live

Love

Laugh

&

Coffee

Other than the coffee, it felt like a mystery how I was to ever do any of the other things.

Approaching the Coroner's Court building, I felt my legs begin to resist taking another step. I so desperately needed to see Jono, but the finality of confirming his death was making my legs feel heavy. I did not want this moment. Guided by my loving family, we slowly made our way into the building. At any other time previously, I would have found it fascinating to be here, but this was the dreaded time. I had attended this building in a previous professional role, but today it did not feel like the same building.

The staff at the Melbourne Coroner's Court are unbelievably amazing. Their gentleness and compassion enabled me, in what was probably the most horrific moment of my life, to enter a space where I felt gently held. After the process was explained to us and we signed the required paperwork, we were guided into a passage with a closed door facing us. The staff member had explained what we would see when she opened the door and led us into that room.

There he was.

Jono lay on what looked like a temporary bed, with a sheet to his neck. My beautiful, wonderful, brilliant son. The screams and sobs that came from somewhere deep down were unrecognisable to me. I wasn't even sure if it was my body they were coming from. Together, arms wrapped around each other, we let out our own expressions of horror. They were totally uninhibited and very raw. I have read somewhere how the pain of the soul reveals itself in moments like this, and that is what was happening to all of us.

Apart from a red mark on his nose (which in other times could easily have resembled a soccer injury) his face was not damaged. My immediate and first response was to 'make it better for him', as my role of a mother was always to help heal the wounds. To bathe it, to dress it, to rub it better. I could do none of those things. I would no longer be able to do this for Jono. He lay there motionless under the sheet. My hands beat against the glass. There was so much I needed to say, I just did not know where to begin.

My daughter told me later of a thought that had crossed her mind. Perhaps, just maybe, the person under the sheet might not actually be Jono. If only that had been so. Instead, we were all there and it was our Jono in front of us. We were trying to say all the things we had not been given time to say before he died. My biggest repeated question was, probably, most obvious. 'WHY? WHY? WHY?'

We sobbed and cried and yelled and released something of what this tragedy had meant to each of us. We said all the things we needed to for that moment. And suddenly, it felt like all my energy had been used. I was an unwilling participant of my soul's sadness. I felt my energy draining, leaving rapidly through my legs. I was becoming aware they could no longer take the weight of my body. My legs were no longer willing to help me stand there.

Two or three steps behind us was a couch, which I was lovingly guided to by my family. We all sat there motionless. The silence seemed almost as loud as our vocalised despair only minutes before.

And then my eldest son said, 'Can you feel it?'

Replacing the noisy, traumatic despair was an unexplainable sense of peace. This was the brief moment of calm. If Jono had been there (and part of me believed he was), I just imagined him saying something like, 'Okay everyone, that's enough now. Just take some deep breaths and relax a little.'

So, we did. We just sat, still able to look at him lying there, still being in his presence, and it felt like to me that I never wanted to leave.

We only had a small allocation of time in that room, so eventually we had to say goodbye. My legs were still very wobbly, having regained only some strength. The very kind staff member offered to provide me with a wheelchair.

My immediate response was, 'No way! Jono would laugh at me if he saw me going out of here in one.'

The support provided by my family enabled me to get out of there and walk back down the long corridor toward the door. I remember thinking that I never ever wanted to step foot inside that building ever again.

Curiously, several months later we were staying in the city with some relatives from New Zealand, and as we walked around the area where our accommodation was, I began feeling something I couldn't describe. I then realised we were only a street away from the Coroner's Court. I find it amazing how our body reacts as it holds onto a memory.

Many years ago, I had a friend whose wife and two daughters died in a horrific car accident. It was an incredibly tough time not only for the family but for everyone who knew them. I recalled the many expenses that were covered by the Transport Accident Compensation (TAC) and felt relieved he didn't have to bear the brunt of the financial burden during this time. What I didn't know was that when someone jumps in front of a train, it is considered a 'pedestrian accident' and there are certain costs TAC also cover.

The caring and attentive people I spoke to at TAC seemed to go above and beyond what was required. They were compassionate and accepting of my tearful voice, articulating clearly how they could help us.

A large majority of the funeral costs were going to be

covered by the TAC, and they would also cover the cost of my daughter returning from London. For an instant, I considered how some of my New Zealand family may be able to be present, but I was told this was only available for immediate family. Later, when the time was right, they would also cover the costs of some counselling if required. Surprisingly, they told me that it is usually the role of the funeral directors to arrange a TAC claim, but for some reason this task was left to us.

Completing paperwork for this was quite an ordeal, but it gave us something to focus on. Whether we liked it or not, it was a task that had to be done. Firstly, we had to obtain a reference number from the train company. In stark contrast to speaking with the TAC, trying to explain to the train company what I required from them could have been almost a comedy had it not been so tragic. When I attempted to explain the situation, I was asked questions such as '... and which direction was the train travelling?' with my response being, 'I'm not sure as I wasn't there'. And then he commented '... but the train doesn't stop at that station', with my response being, 'well it did that day.'

Finally, following a rather distorted conversation, and being put on hold for lengthy periods, uncertain as to what he was doing, we were given a reference number. I was then able to pass this on to the TAC.

There were several unexpected tasks to complete in the aftermath of Jono's death, and this was one of them. Whoever considers all the aspects involved following someone jumping in front of a train? Fortunately, this is information not many people need to know. I thought, having been a social worker, a death doula and a funeral celebrant, that I might have a capacity to navigate all these tasks with much more clarity than what I had been doing. I was jolted into understanding during this process, that when death becomes a personal experience, it becomes something different altogether.

As I worked in the death/dying/funeral area, I was well informed of the sorts of funerals currently available. As previously mentioned, from the time I was told of Jono's death, a particular funeral director came to mind because of contact I had already had with them. I was adamant we had to use them to help farewell Jono because it was, after all, going to be his last big hurrah. So, phone calls were made and meetings arranged. Plans were made for the funeral arranger to come to our home.

The morning of the funeral planning meeting, we, as a family, were sitting around the dining room table with our coffees, discussing aspects of the funeral. Perry, who was busy sweeping the floor in the adjacent room, suddenly turned up the volume of a song that was playing on the radio. It was the Bull sisters (Vika and Linda) singing 'Bridge Over Troubled Water'. Silence fell around the table as we listened to each word of that song, almost as though we were hearing them for the first time. We all felt Jono's presence, and he was offering us love. We were all very tearful, but in a beautifully connected way. Somehow, it felt like these words were caressing our hearts. We knew then that this was one song we would need to include in his funeral.

Along with the funeral arranger, around twelve or thirteen of us sat in our lounge room that evening, trying desperately to imagine how we could do justice to Jono's life at his final farewell. We were committed to honouring Jono in a way that he would consider fitting and appropriate. He was such a committed lawyer who continually fought for justice. We wanted him to be proud of our arrangements. We had already been warned by one of his close friends and colleagues to expect a very large gathering. It was becoming obvious to us that Jono had collected many people in his short life. A venue large enough to hold this funeral had to be found so it wouldn't exclude anyone who wanted to come and farewell their friend. There were several places that could accommodate 300 to 400 people, so we chose a place in Northcote and a venue he had previously attended socially. Throughout the several hours it took to put plans in place, there continued to be moments of utter disbelief. How could it be that we were planning a funeral for our beautiful, vibrant, full of life Jono? It was unfathomable.

It almost sounds impossible to say this, but there were lighter moments spattered throughout that planning evening. There were times when someone would say something that Jono may have said or done in that situation that brought some laughter. Contrary to that, we were also feeling the heavy weight of Jono. It was as though he was feeling so sad that we had to arrange this. I tried to imagine a potential conversation he and I may have had a few weeks previously, if I had been describing such a funeral planning meeting to him, as part of my role as a celebrant. I knew he would have been so sad and felt deep compassion for the family. We all sat there that night and felt Jono's sadness, along with our own.

And then the funeral planning was done. Well, perhaps I should say we had the bones of it worked out. Now we had to fill in all the gaps. We had nominated who should speak during the funeral and what kind of format it should take and who the pallbearers would be and who would accompany him to the crematorium at Fawkner. That aspect of the planning was complete. We now had to decide what he was going to be dressed in, what photos were going to be used, what of his favourite music would be on the playlist, and what each of us were going to say.

In between the planning, we somehow had to tend to everyday tasks. All those little things, like trying to sleep, trying to eat, choosing which clothes to put on each day, was a challenge. Every movement was difficult. It did not help that we seemed to endure day after day with grey skies and so much rain. The sky kept crying and it felt like we had not seen the sun for so long. Perhaps our hearts would be forever overcast and grey and we would always be as sad as the skies above. I was told once there is deep wisdom to be found in sadness. Perhaps one day I may be able to access that wisdom.

My daughter and I both agreed we would go shopping to

Chapter Four   The padlock of love

buy a new outfit to wear to Jono's funeral. He would have expected that of us. My problem was that I had become more and more of an op shop buyer of clothes. I was challenged by the amount of money I knew I would have to spend on something brand new, compared to what I would normally buy! But I did know that Jono was encouraging me to step up and choose something specific to wear on his special day.

Over the previous few years, I had struggled going into shopping centres, as I think we have become such a consumer-orientated society. Jono and I had shared similar thoughts on this. So understandably, as my daughter and I started to explore Chadstone Shopping Centre, a large and somewhat expensive mecca for fashion, I felt little enthusiasm in my search for clothes.

I had noticed since Jono died that any decision-making had become extremely difficult. The fog in my brain and the hurt in my heart had been encroaching on my day-to-day tasks. I still felt as though I was somehow being carried through each day without fully participating in it.

My daughter found her choice reasonably quickly, and I wondered if I would find anything that I felt comfortable with. Finally, in one shop, I chose around four dresses to try on. As hard as it was, I had decided not to look at any of the price tags; instead, I would choose the one that 'felt right'. Yes, finally my daughter and I both agreed on a blue dress. It felt comfortable, and I knew I would probably be able to wear it again (although two years down the track, at the time of writing, I'm not sure how I will ever be able to put it on again). So, regardless of the cost, this was going to be my choice. The big reveal of the price had us both in stitches of laughter (and we could hear Jono there with us) as it was the cheapest of all my choices and was on special with a 50% discount!

I stood at the counter as the shop assistant scanned my card, and she asked me if I wanted it wrapped or in a bag. It was as though she was speaking a foreign language, and all I could do was look at her. It felt impossible to decide how my new purchase would be carried. I felt stunned as I looked at her, and she repeated her question. My response was something like, 'whatever you want'. In that moment, I wondered whether my decision-making confidence would ever return. The trauma I was experiencing from my son's unexpected death felt crippling. This was the antithesis of who I had known myself to be.

Tuesday, 7 June 2022, would have been the day Jono celebrated turning 32. We considered what we could or should do to recognise this day. Part of me wanted to just sleep through it, but instead we chose to have a birthday party for Jono, just five days after he died.

We decided the right thing to do was to cook all his favourite foods and invite his closest friends to come and share his birthday celebration with us. Jono really enjoyed the recipes from the great chef Yotam Ottolenghi, so most of the food we prepared came from those cookbooks. All except for a fish pie

Chapter Four The padlock of love

I had cooked for him only four or five weeks before, which he had declared was the best fish pie he had ever had. I made his favourite chocolate cake and his three nieces iced it with soccer balls. We tried as hard as we could to invoke his spirit, along with his joy and his love, to be present with us all on that day.

There were around 25 people who came to Jono's birthday party, and everyone was encouraged to share stories and memories of Jono.

The memory most vivid for me was when we celebrated his 21st in Florence. As previously mentioned, he spent time studying at the University of Prato. His sister and I joined him for the week of his birthday. We went to an authentic Italian café in Florence, along with several of his Australian student friends. He had told me earlier that he now thought birthday cakes were only for children, and he no longer enjoyed the idea of everyone focussing on him to sing 'Happy Birthday'. While I disagreed with him, I acknowledged and accepted his comment. During our dessert orders being taken, the waiter inquired if we were all a table of students. I was flattered, but I replied that I was Jono's mum, who had come to visit to celebrate his 21st birthday. As they brought out our deserts, the lights were dimmed, and there on Jono's desert was a candle and all those who were present in the café sang 'Happy Birthday' to him! I had a difficult time convincing him that I had no idea that was going to happen.

Back in Australia, in June of 2022, we toasted Jono on what would have been his 32nd birthday. The afternoon was filled with tears alongside laughter and lots of love. Many of us who were present could certainly feel the essence of Jono in the room. He loved all the people present and never missed a gathering like this, despite the fact he may not have enjoyed being the centre of attention.

I really missed Jono's presence that day and I could still not fully comprehend he had died. In my heart, I knew there were so many other people missing him too and I just wanted to extend my love to all the many others who were also missing him, including his colleagues.

Jono's workplace was deeply affected by his death. It appeared he was as much loved by the people I didn't know as the ones I did know. The CEO of the law firm had contacted us to let us know they were going to have a gathering at the end of the next day for his close friends within the firm. They were going to gather and debrief on what had happened. He asked if we, Jono's family, would like to be present.

Without any hesitation, we said how much we would appreciate being there. A taxi was arranged by them to transport us into the city. None of us were feeling particularly robust enough to navigate city driving and parking, so it was a relief to be collected and dropped off. As we were driven through the city streets, getting closer to his place of work, I was filled with so much pain. This was where he came every day, and this was his world that we were not actually a part of. Just as I was thinking it, Tony said, 'I keep looking at all

Chapter Four   The padlock of love

the people walking the streets and thinking we should be seeing Jono there. This is where he should be.' Instead, he would never walk those streets again. This vibrant city that he loved, this city where he knew all the best coffee places, and all the best sushi places, would never again hear his footsteps.

We alighted from the maxi-cab and were met by staff members from Jono's firm. Some of these people had known Jono for many years. They were taking us to meet the CEO, who would then take us to the board room where other colleagues were already gathered. It felt like we were entering new territory. I had visited his office before, but not since they had relocated a few years ago. There was no sense of familiarity to us, but just knowing that this was the lift that Jono caught every day, and these were steps he had taken so many times, was crushing. We were reminded he had walked this floor for the last time.

We were warmly greeted by the CEO, who, like us, was also in shock over Jono's death. By now, we were now starting to understand that Jono had affected just about everyone he had met more than twice. He told us that Jono's close colleagues were already gathered in the board room and invited us to follow him. I did know some of Jono's close work friends, and in my mind thought we might walk into a room of ten or fifteen people.

As we approached the boardroom, we could hear quite a large crowd of voices chattering and were shocked to walk into a room of about seventy people. As five of us from the family walked into the room, immediate silence fell as they realised we had arrived. I could not help myself, questioning what Jono would have done in a situation such as this, and said, 'Wow, I know we are a special family, but I don't think we have ever had this effect on a group of people!'

I felt I needed to 'break the ice' and for them to be comfortable knowing that while we were a deeply grieving family, we could also dip into Jono's sense of humour when needed.

Most people struggle to know what to say when speaking with bereaved family members. I talk about this in more detail in later chapters, but on this day, I'm sure there were many people there who felt uncertain as to what to say to us. They were also struggling to believe Jono had died. We had come to hear about Jono's work life and how he impacted those that knew him. I found myself offering so many people an opportunity to share their own grief as we both cried. There was such a depth of compassion and empathy that was mutually exchanged during our visit.

We heard so many stories from so many people about how amazing Jono had been at work. So many people considered him to be in their close circle of friends. So many people told us how Jono was such an amazing lawyer. We heard about his pro bono work. We heard about how he made sure people remained connected during the COVID-19 lockdowns. We also heard about his attendance at a work conference on the Gold Coast, less than a week previously. He had won a game of poker on the Thursday night and participated in the final

Chapter Four   The padlock of love

night costume party, with the team (including Jono) dressed in the characters of 101 Dalmatians. And within a week, he had taken his own life. No wonder his work colleagues were asking as many 'why' questions as we were.

Following the gathering we asked to be taken to Jono's office so we could stand in his space. As we approached his office, the staff member accompanying us told us we might be surprised, as many people had left floral tributes.

Wow ... I thought we had received so many flowers, and now there seemed just as many here in his workspace. He had received so many tributes from people within his professional life, including competing law firms. I sat in his chair and looked out the window and down nine floors to a busy street. I knew this was where he did such good things for the world. I felt such a sense of pride that a slight smile warmed my soul, knowing how pleased he was with his work. This was where he should still have been. No matter how wrong it was, he wasn't there. Instead, in his place were many written and floral tributes to such an amazing lawyer, friend, and great human.

We sat mostly in silence on the trip home, trying to digest the impact that our wonderful Jono had on all those he encountered. I tried hard to understand how deeply he was going to be missed within the legal world. I wondered how long his work colleagues would miss him. Would it be two years, or ten years, or perhaps his name may still be written somewhere in fifteen years? For me, I have been given a 'forever' sentence.

I know, for the rest of my life, there is a huge hole that can never be filled.

Our family spoke later that night about trying to guess what was on his mind on that Thursday morning. What had led him to make that dreadful decision to dive in front of that train? Each of us had our own ideas of what he may have been thinking. At times like these, people try their hardest to make some kind of sense of the chaos surrounding them. I remember as we gathered in one of our many locked arm circles of love, our padlock of love, I said, 'One day—not today—we may have to accept the fact that we may never know with certainty what Jono was thinking before he jumped. And we may have to learn to live with that unknown.'

Chapter Five
The vigil and the funeral

The funeral arranger had offered the family a place and time to spend with Jono before the funeral. Initially, I was hesitant, as that would require some embalming. Being on the committee of Natural Death Advocacy Network (NDAN) I preferred things to be as natural as possible. I felt that his once beautiful body had already been through enough. I was, however, reminded on many occasions that this was not just about what I wanted. There were other people to take into consideration as well. The immediate family had seen him at the Coroner's Court, but I was told by the funeral arranger there were also others who wanted to see him for one last time.

So, against my initial wishes, the vigil was arranged for the night before his funeral.

The space was rather beautiful, but walking in the front door and seeing the un-lidded pine enviro coffin several metres in front of us stopped me in my tracks. We had arrived together as a family and had already agreed to give ourselves permission to take all the time we needed. I slowly walked towards him; with each step I saw more of Jono. With the history of my work, and the number of personal deaths I had already experienced, I had seen many dead people. Often, they look nothing like they did when they were alive because of all the mortuary work done. Looking at Jono, I was comforted to see he looked just like Jono. He had always taken pride in how he dressed and looked; and I knew he would be pleased with his appearance lying ever so peacefully in that coffin. I smiled as I gently touched his hand and kissed him on the forehead. I could almost say I felt his approval. It was as though he was preparing to receive his guests, and as such, he was.

Other friends of Jono had also been invited to the vigil, so I prepared myself for facing his friends. It wasn't long before they started arriving to spend their last moments with Jono. There were lots of hugs and tears shared by many. A great musical playlist had been chosen, and throughout the following hour or so, some of us started writing messages on his coffin. I had also written a letter to him, as other family members had, and we placed them next to him in the coffin. Tony had worn an Arsenal scarf to honour Jono's football team and asked me if I thought he should also place that in the coffin. Of course it was his decision, but it felt like it would be a comfort to Jono as he tucked it in beside him.

I had the opportunity during the evening to reconnect with some of Jono's friends I hadn't seen for quite some time and to meet some new friends. We were there because we all loved Jono. We were there to share our grief. We were there because being connected in grief can be soothing. 'Doing grief' is not something that should ever happen in isolation. Connected souls have a strong need to come together and feel and share the pain of loss.

Once his friends had left, we, as a family, enjoyed having the space to ourselves for the last fifteen minutes. We popped some champagne and toasted Jono. He would be forever in our hearts, but we were there to see the physical Jono for the last time. How we had seen him that night was how we would always remember him.

He would never grow old.

Forever 31.

Two weeks after Jono died was the day of his funeral. This time frame is now becoming a common wait time for funerals. During that two week period, we had an opportunity to try to settle our chaotic minds and offer each other loving arms and tissues when needed. There were still a lot of people coming and going and the energy in my home was something I had never experienced before. The difficulty in describing it is because there was such deep love present, and yet it was mixed with such deep sadness. I could almost describe it as electric, but not even that would do it justice.

I was glad to have had the time in between when he died and the funeral. The advantage of this two weeks gave us time to consider in more detail how we would farewell Jono. While the trauma was still ever present, it allowed space in between the event and the funeral. The disadvantage of this time lapse meant delaying the final act for Jono. It reminded me of when children fall and scrape their knees. The bleeding stops fairly soon, and slowly the skin begins to repair itself. Suddenly a child's inquisitive mind leads them to scratch the scar and the bleeding starts all over again. The funeral, two weeks later, felt as though we had scratched off the scar.

We hired a small bus for the day which allowed all the immediate family to travel together. We each felt strongly connected and had a need to remain close. We kept reminding ourselves we could do this day together. Our commitment was to honour Jono. A family friend offered to drive the bus. This friend collected the bus at 9:00 am in the morning and didn't drop us home until around 7:15 pm. We had received such an incredible gift of time and support. I was reminded that angels appear in a variety of ways in this world.

It was about an hour's drive to the venue we had chosen to mourn the loss of and celebrate Jono's life. It was a reasonably silent and sombre trip. How does a mother, or for that matter, any family member, prepare themselves both emotionally and physically to attend the funeral of their youngest son? In one sense I wanted to hold on to this day forever because after this his body would be gone. Right now, we still had his body here on earth with us. I had read and tried hard to believe that 'those we love don't go away—they walk beside us every day'. I so hoped that would be true as I never wanted to stop feeling Jono in my life.

As we walked into the Greenhouse, an appropriately named venue, at around 11:30 am, my heart skipped a beat as I saw

Chapter Five The vigil and the funeral

Jono's coffin again. This time the lid was on, but I knew my beautiful boy was inside. Alongside him were the notes and scarf we had placed with him the previous evening. All those who were gathering were invited to draw or write a message to Jono on his coffin. It gave people something to do. So many loving messages and images covered his coffin. I only hoped that what people were writing were things they had already told Jono. I hope he knew before he died just how many people loved and cared for him.

So many people, many of whom I had never previously met, kept arriving. More and more people arrived until that room had met its maximum occupancy of 300. The venue had set up a screen to watch and hear the funeral in the adjacent bar which held around another 100. When that was filled, we were told later that there were about another 100 people out on the street. Again and again we were reminded that Jono was a highly respected colleague and much-loved friend. In addition to the people physically present, there were 150 devices connected to the live stream. I knew many of my New Zealand family were watching and I was told later that one of those devices had 200 people watching from a boardroom. Jono's impact on the world was almost overwhelming.

My nephew, a well-known Melbourne jazz musician, opened the gathering with an amazing improvisation on his keyboard. It provided an opportunity to breathe deeply and prepare to go to a deep place. Each note he played reverberated within my soul.

The funeral celebrant began this time by acknowledging Jono's ancestors from both Tony and me, and inviting them to be present, and telling us that Jono was now one of our ancestors as well.

In the days before the funeral, the celebrant had requested dot points about Jono from many people, including family and friends. She then collected them and presented a combined story about who our son was and what he meant to so many people.

We then listened, for almost an hour, to the many things that had been said about the person Jono: a son, a brother, an uncle, a cousin, a nephew, and a much-loved friend. There were tears and laughter combined. Jono had a very keen sense of humour, and this became more and more evident from the many memories recalled.

And then it was our turn. Tony, myself, Jono's brother, his sister, and his niece (my 26-year-old granddaughter) all wanted this opportunity to share stories of the person he was. We stood together as one combined unit. We had chosen to wear one of Jono's ties as a symbol of him standing with us. When I started to speak, I drew strength from that tie.

As a funeral celebrant myself, I knew the convention was to suggest that people speak no longer than four minutes and generally there would be no more than three or four speakers for each funeral. This is usually based on the time constraints of any given venue, and the time pressure from the funeral directors. Today, the professional became personal, and we were going to have as long as we all needed. We had exclusive access to the venue until 4:00 pm.

Each family member had not shared with the others what they had written, but it was so beautifully woven; our love, our pain, our gritty grief, our sadness and even our humour created the most amazing tapestry of a life well lived in such a short time.

We had asked significant others to also share their tributes to Jono. There were five more speakers, concluding with his boss, who was also moved to tears, telling the world how much Jono was going to be missed.

Jono's sister had made an incredible video of Jono's life. Many people had been invited to share their photos, in addition to the hundreds we had. This video started with the song 'Bridge Over Troubled Water' and evoked the same feelings as the morning we had heard it on the radio sitting around our table. We watched photos of Jono from a baby right up until the week before he died. We could almost hear his laughter and see his flailing his arms as he tried to make a point. We saw his life flash before our eyes.

More than two hours after we walked into the Greenhouse it was time for him to leave. My daughter and I walked behind those who lovingly carried him to the waiting hearse. It felt like a very long walk, and yet there was that very familiar part of me that did not want it to stop. I wanted to walk behind him forever.

As we walked out to the busyness of High Street, Northcote,

it felt like the whole world had stopped to say goodbye to Jono. I noticed on the footpath a rather gorgeous dog just sitting and waiting for the procession to clear so he could continue his walk. Jono loved dogs, and this dog looked similar to our dog Pepa, who had died ten years before. Perry was also drawn to this dog, waiting patiently, and took a photo of him. How surprised we were when we looked closely at that photo much later to see his name tag said Bowie. Jono had held a keen interest in David Bowie. Can we call these things coincidences? I'm not sure I believe in coincidences anymore. Since Jono died, I have experienced so many coincidences that now I accept them as being something from the next dimension, and that often we are not meant to fully understand what they mean. Perhaps we just have to accept them.

I wasn't sure I would ever be ready for the back door of that wonderful old Cadillac to be closed. My hand felt as though it was sealed to the lid of the coffin with glue. Eventually, I took a step back as they closed the rear door and I watched the white 1973 Cadillac Deville head down High Street, taking my son on his final trip. His last ride was to the Fawkner Crematorium. His father and sister sat in the front with the driver, taking the last ride with him.

Again, I felt that now familiar feeling of energy draining from my body. It was leaving my legs very unsteady and it felt as though they were refusing to bear the weight of my pain. I fell into the arms of my supportive (in more ways than one) daughter-in-law and granddaughter, as they gently helped me back inside to a seat.

Jono had gone. The structured part of the day was complete. Now we could eat, drink, share informal stories, and honour the empty space that Jono left.

Sometimes, it is in the messiest parts of our life that we are most human. I had never felt in such a mess and questioned how it would ever be possible for it feel any different. Was this feeling, the feeling of being at my most human? Jono's absence seemed to be everywhere I looked.

If I'm honest, the rest of the afternoon is a blurry memory. I remember snippets, like having a cup of tea brought to me, along with a glass of water, some champagne, and a glass of red wine all arriving at the same time! Some people feel uncomfortable with mess, and want to tidy it up, but I think I was given some exemptions that day to continue being messy as long as I needed to.

There were many conversations had that day, some remaining in my memory. I remember the beautiful words spoken by the judge that Jono had worked with as he praised his efforts as his associate several years previously. He finished his conversation saying, 'The one thing I can say about Jono is that he hid his depressive disorder well.' My reply was, 'That is because he did not have one. He was not depressed. He had a glitch.'

Speaking to a Federal Court judge using less than technical medical terminology appeared to take him a little by surprise, as he responded with, 'Oh...?' I could almost hear Jono beside me, strongly suggesting that was no way to speak to a judge!

Later in the book I suggest the many ways suicide can be viewed, but one thing I know for sure is that not everyone will have depression before they suicide. Sometimes people make spur of the moment decisions, and we that are left behind call them mistakes. More on that soon.

There were many of Jono's school and university friends present that day. It was so sad that it took this event to finally reconnect with them again. More stories and memories were shared, mixed with laughter and tears. When I recollect that day, there is a part of me that wishes I could have recorded all those conversations, to be kept forever. Instead, I'm afraid my memory will slowly let them go.

Just before the wake finished, I was approached by several of Jono's work colleagues who presented me with a beautiful black tribute book. Inside were all the messages they had received for Jono, including all the cards that had been on the floral tributes in his office. Page after page was filled with messages about how Jono had been there for them; how he had offered friendship and support to so many; how many people considered him a close friend. It was almost overwhelming, but it was such a treasure to have. If I didn't know before today, I now had confirmed just how many lives Jono had touched and how many people were going to miss him.

We all clambered into the bus, feeling like very different people than when we had alighted earlier that day. We had

Chapter Five The vigil and the funeral

farewelled our beloved Jono. Life from this point would be very different; our love for and from Jono would be felt in a different way. The one thing I hold onto is knowing it will never stop.

On the trip home I reflected on funerals generally and it suddenly occurred to me that no one is ever fully known by another until they die. By that, I mean that we all had our own unique relationship with Jono, but it was only within the context of our individual relationship that we knew him. None of his family had a way of knowing who he was to all the other people in his life. I may have had a relationship with Jono for 31 years and 360 days, and along with Tony and our other children, I had known him much longer than most others at his funeral. As I sat listening to the overwhelming tributes of friendship and fairness and justice and kindness that so many others expressed, I learned more about Jono that day than ever before. Each person told the story of their relationship with Jono which totally expanded on the relationship I had with him. It felt like I was able to see Jono from a whole new and enhanced perspective.

It made me consider why, in our society, we nominate the position of the family as the chief mourners when I heard that day of so many relationships of friendship and kindness that Jono had shared with so many others. The searing pain and loss of Jono that others were experiencing was surely deserving of their position as equal mourners.

I felt as though I now had a deeper insight into the impact

my Jono had on the world. It made his indescribable death even more tragic, knowing he would no longer be able to physically contribute. I could not help but think of the many lives Jono would have touched, both in friendships and in the legal systems, had he not died. I wondered how many hundreds of lives had missed out on having Jono in their lives.

Another revelation that came to me on the way home that day was the importance of moments that had taken place before the funeral. The funeral, I then realised, did not appear to be the only place for us a family to grieve. It occurred to me that the 'moments' we had all shared before the funeral were significant in our grieving leading up to this day. Firstly, we as a family had seen his body at the Coroner's Office; then we had gathered at his workplace with his much loved colleagues; then we had gathered to discuss the funeral; then we shared his birthday with friends and family; and finally, before his funeral, we had been part of the vigil with his open coffin. All those moments now felt as though they were steps leading us to the crescendo which was the funeral. I was now able to appreciate the two week gap since his death even more.

I also wondered how I would continue to live without my youngest child.

Chapter Six
Walking the traumatic grief path

It didn't take long for all the makeshift beds to be cleared and all the linen to be washed and packed away. My daughter and her family returned to the UK and somehow life had to continue. For the first time I had space to consider how I was feeling while searching for any familiar grief experiences I could draw from that might provide comfort.

Over the next few months, there were going to be tasks related to Jono's death that required me to be present. Some days I just wanted to stay in bed all day, but I knew this would not be helpful for me or those around me. I could always hear Jono's gentle encouragement in my head, encouraging me to keep going. It gave me time to consider grief generally, realising that traumatic grief can be confusing.

My mother had died from an unexpected heart attack when I was twelve, so I was familiar with significant loss in my life. Since then, my dad, my step-mum, both parents-in-law, all my aunties and uncles, several very close friends and my sister and brother-in-law had died. I even wondered if my early experience of my mother dying had some influence on my choosing to work in the death and dying field. I began working in community-based palliative care in 1999 and had remained in touch with either the death and dying or bereavement field in various roles ever since. I completed my Honours Degree in Social Work and chose to do my research on the lived experience of grief, which was also the title of my thesis, so I was familiar with many theories about grief and had read oh so many books on the subject.

Following Jono's death, I questioned all the knowledge and theory I knew. I felt my current experience had nothing to do with what I was familiar with. I had taught about grief and supported bereaved people for many years. It now felt very different. I told myself all the textbooks would need to be rewritten because very little reflected what I was feeling! The grief-work hypothesis no longer made sense to me. I will discuss grief theories in more depth in an upcoming chapter.

Then it occurred to me that what I was currently experiencing was *trauma*. I felt like I had been assaulted with a strong, blunt instrument. My whole being felt it. I intuitively knew this sense of trauma required further exploration before I could even consider responding to my grief. It felt like I was in emergency mode, almost waiting for the next catastrophic event.

I recall a couple of days before the funeral when we heard our local siren calling volunteers to the Country Fire Authority (CFA) station. I looked on the Emergency app which confirmed they were attending a road accident close to our house. Right at that moment we were waiting for our eldest son to return home and when he didn't answer his mobile phone, I became close to hysterical. My thought, at that point, was if my youngest son had died, then no one in the family was safe from death. Eventually he phoned me back, confirming he was safe. Looking back now, my response was quite normal for the trauma space I was in. It felt like I was in a heightened arousal mode almost continually, and I didn't know when this would end, if indeed it ever would.

What I know now is that when I acknowledged my traumatic experience and learned to accept that my response to trauma was present in my day-to-day life, I accepted that it may take time before I felt differently. When I accepted that, I lost all expectation of being 'fixed'.

I had to accept that while trauma and grief were closely linked, I could not truly attend to my grief needs until I fully understood my trauma response. Not all grief carries trauma and I now realised I was trying to match my previous grief experiences with what I was feeling for Jono. I then knew that trauma has a huge impact on grief. I remember telling someone that if it had been inevitable that Jono was going to die, I would have much rather had the opportunity to care for him with an illness. I would have had the opportunity to say goodbye to him and then felt the heavy weight of grief. Instead, I felt the inexplicable trauma of trying to accept something that made no sense.

There was no way of 'fixing' this. Instead, I recognised that what I had been through from the moment I was told of

Jono's death was incredibly distressing, and my reaction to this trauma was to be expected. I knew that slowly, when the time was right, I would need to confront what had actually happened, despite my desire to sometimes simply block it out. I knew that grief would be with me forever, but I hoped that the trauma I was experiencing would slowly give way to a more even equilibrium. I remember from what I had learnt that relaxation, expressing my feelings fully and trying to confront tough feelings when they arose, would, in the end, lead to reducing my trauma response. I could then explore my own way of grieving for Jono.

There were moments during this time when I wondered if I could continue to live without Jono. I began to overthink the burden of my trauma and grief on other people around me. More than once I thought about leaving this earth myself. I did not know how I could kill myself in a gentle way, and I would always return to the thought that my family had already been through enough.

Once our home returned to its previous state, I had time to sit. I spent many hours sitting in a chair we affectionately refer to as the 'healing chair'. It is positioned in the sun most of the day and looks out on the trees and the hills. It is very comfortable, especially when it's reclined. Sometimes, as I sat, my mind was blank and all I could focus on was my breathing. Other times, I spent quietly crying. My tears were always so present or close to the surface. After a few weeks,

I thought my crying might lessen a little. It didn't, and it seemed there was this bottomless well from wherever my tears came. Even at the time of writing, my tears are always close-by, and I have accepted them and feel okay with that. That's how it is for the now. It might change or it might not. I am comforted by the thought that my tears water the garden of my soul. I have noticed that my crying seems much more of a problem for others than it is for me.

I found a comforting quote from Washington Irving, an American 19th century author:

There is a sacredness in tears. They are not the mark of weakness, but of power. They speak more eloquently than ten thousand tongues. They are the messengers of overwhelming grief, of deep contrition and of unspeakable love.

When people contacted me and wanted to arrange a meet-up, I would always say, 'I cry a lot these days, so I hope you are comfortable with that.' When friends and neighbours ask questions about Jono and my tears come to the surface, they often say, 'Oh, I'm sorry, I've made you cry.' My response is always, 'You haven't made me cry. I cry because Jono is dead, not because we are talking about him.' It is so important for me to be able to continually speak of Jono. I need people to be okay with my tears without trying to stop me crying, or apologising for 'making me cry'. All I ask is for people to feel comfortable sitting with me in my pain and to keep speaking Jono's name.

On a lighter note, there are advantages of tears being frequently present. Over the last few years, I had been suffering from dry eye syndrome, requiring eye drops every day. Since Jono died, my abundance of my natural tears means I have not used drops once!

I don't believe crying should ever measure whether someone is doing okay or not. Even though, as a celebrant, I have been able to compartmentalise my emotions while being present at funerals, I find myself freely crying over sad movies. It is no wonder then, that since Jono's death, I have accepted that I cry easily. This does not mean I am 'stuck' or 'in trouble with my grief', it simply means I cry a lot. Having said that, there are some people who can't or don't cry, and this means nothing more or less, except that we are all different and have unique responses to situations.

There were events in my life that were going to happen, despite the fact it felt like the world should just stop. I'm going to describe some of those now, but throughout all of them, my crying, or sometimes just tears, remained close to me.

The coroner was concerned enough about the nature and unexpected death of Jono that he chose to further investigate. As a family, we were pleased with this, hoping the inquiry may shed some further light on what happened. We always felt there were missing parts in our knowledge, and we were left with many questions leading up to his time of death. We hoped further investigation could provide some answers that we all felt would bring much relief. Not knowing what went through Jono's mind in the hours leading to his death had kept me awake for many nights.

A coronial investigation meant the police requested an interview with me as I had some of the last phone conversations with Jono in the days before he died. Fortunately, I was able to take Perry with me and we attended one of our local police stations. Apart from reporting a lost wallet many years ago, I had never been interviewed by a police officer and was a little unsure of what to expect.

Two caring policewomen conducted the interview. I wasn't fully prepared for the depth of questioning, but they managed it with so much kindness and compassion that it lessened any sense of intrusive questioning. Part of me wanted to provide all that I could to assist with the coroner in gaining further understanding about Jono's death, but another part wondered how I could speak of such intimate details with complete strangers. At moments when I glimpsed tears in their eyes, I felt so sorry for the job they had. One thing I was learning about this experience, is the more I spoke about Jono, and what had taken place leading up to his death, the more it helped me to believe that he wasn't coming back. These were the kind of moments when it made it more real.

Four and a half hours after beginning the interview, I had answered all the questions and we were free to leave.

I was completely exhausted, and walking down the steps toward our car that familiar feeling of my legs not wanting to work returned. Perry helped guide me back to the car where I just sat. I had told the police about Jono's entire life, including the last few phone calls when he was questioning everything. We were no closer to knowing what had happened in the last twelve hours of his life. I kept reminding myself that we may never know, and therein lay the pain and the truth. I wondered if I had not gone to New Zealand, and instead listened to my intuition, would he still be alive? If I had been here, he may have reached out to me. Was I somehow implicated in his death because I wasn't in the same country when he needed me the most? No matter how irrational, or rational, these thoughts were, I could not stop them. It was as though they were on a loop.

When I had completed the interview, I was curious about how many other people the police needed to interview to gain an overall perspective. One of the people I was curious about was the person who was driving the train that Jono jumped in front of. I didn't know how someone could cope with the sort of work trauma that the driver had experienced on 2 June 2022. I had heard it was common for train drivers to receive support for these sorts of incidences, but I continued to think about him. I spoke with Tony about this, and we both decided, as Jono's parents, we would write a letter to him to let him know a little more about Jono. We wanted to apologise on behalf of Jono, as we knew, in his normal life, he would never willingly inflict this traumatic experience on anyone. Together, we wrote a letter to that driver with the hope it may have offered some further healing. We later discovered that after seventeen years of train driving this was his third fatality. My compassion enveloped him. It was important for me to share with him some knowledge of who Jono was, and that we believed this split-second decision was a mistake. I hope that letter made some difference for that driver. We never heard anything in reply.

It was around this time that I began to consider whether I should seek some external help. I knew many grief counsellors, and having been one myself, I was hesitant in reaching out. I wondered if there was anything at all that could lessen my overwhelm. I found it difficult to draw on any of my previous clinical knowledge and felt conflicted in even considering whether anything at all could help the way I was feeling. I knew what I did not want. I did not want someone to offer me platitudes, or even present a theoretical approach to my grief, as I already knew all the theories in my head and they didn't seem to help.

Despite my uncertainty, I thought professional help might offer me something, and if after one visit I didn't feel any benefit, then I didn't need to return. Once I made the decision to seek help, I decided it would be more beneficial to see someone I didn't know. I felt fortunate in knowing that I still had the capacity to apply my research skills to find the psychologist I thought would meet my needs. I hesitatingly made my first appointment.

My first visit to them was on the same day I had to officiate at my first wedding since Jono's death. I had told the couple what had happened and offered them another celebrant, but they had formed a relationship with me and were very keen to support me in my role as their celebrant. Given it was only about six weeks since Jono's death, I felt I conducted the ceremony beautifully. It was small, intimate and very meaningful.

I went straight to the psychologist from the wedding. They were so welcoming and had no expectations of me. I felt accepted. What comforted me greatly was the disclosure of a suicide death in their extended family, some time ago. I knew then they would know something of the agony and the unanswered questions that plagued me. To tell the story all over again took nearly a whole box of tissues. This was okay, because I felt I was in a place where I didn't need to apologise for my emotion. I knew I had connected with them, and following that first visit I felt a relief and a knowledge that I had been supported by someone who was totally removed from the situation. I knew there would be benefit in this. I knew I had made the right decision to seek help and there would be future visits.

It felt like anything I did totally depleted me of energy in the weeks following Jono's death. I knew there were daily tasks that were necessary, but a part of me wanted to escape the trauma of what was now my daily existence. I found my usual practice of meditation and relaxation almost impossible to even consider. Even my daily walks, which I had been told would be beneficial, felt beyond me. During this 'impossible time' something I found helpful was breathing. Mostly we do this automatically, without giving much thought to the process, but when I sat and focussed on my breathing, it provided some respite from my thoughts. Breathing was not optional! I had learnt the positive effect of deep breathing in many workshops and although I hadn't always remembered to use it, now was the time to call it in.

Without becoming too technical, our breathing is part of our body's response to stress. If we use deep breathing more often, sometimes referred to as 'diaphragmatic' breathing, we may see that our stress levels lower. It has even been proved scientifically. The practice of deep breathing not only lowers stress levels, it can also be beneficial to our overall wellness, including lowering blood pressure. The best part about it is that it is free and accessible.

Most of us breathe from our chest and keep our breaths quite shallow, but when we take deep breaths, it enables more air flow into our bodies and helps us to find calm. I recall in the hours and days that followed Jono's death I would often have the feeling I was unable to breathe. During this time, I was very aware that I was breathing very quickly and with short, shallow breaths. This was how my nervous system was reacting. No one reminded me to take some deep breaths, so in my times of stress I continued to breathe quickly.

Deep breathing involves breathing from your stomach. As you breathe in, imagine it going way past your lungs and deep within your stomach. Place your hand on your stomach and feel it filling with your breath; as you exhale, feel your stomach push all that air out.

I would find myself sitting for long periods and often I would lower my shoulders and focus on my breath. I would sit and imagine myself following my breath, from the moment I breathed in, feeling it in my nostrils and travelling with it as it reached my belly. Then, as I exhaled, I would imagine following it again as it totally left my body. I would take around four seconds to breathe in, holding it in place for four seconds, and then another four seconds to release it. Most people are familiar with the phrase 'just take a deep breath' when being faced with challenging moments. I was reminded that it really does help.

I also needed to be around people I loved. They offered calm and moments of distraction from my continual reminders of Jono's death. My eldest son would visit regularly and being enveloped by his arms, hugging me tight, was so very reassuring.

However, I was missing my daughter and her family, as they had now returned to London. Much earlier in 2022, I had made flight bookings to be with my daughter in the UK for the month of August. Her girls would be in their summer break, and I thought it would be so amazing to catch up with them all after such a long stretch of COVID-19 lockdowns. Seeing

Chapter Six   Walking the traumatic grief path

them when they returned to Australia for Jono's funeral was obviously unexpected. So now I had to decide if I would still go to London in August. After some thought and lots of discussion, there was no doubt I still needed to be with my daughter, more than ever before. Cautiously, I continued my plans to arrive in the UK on the 29th of July.

I visit the UK regularly and love flying, but I could not muster up my regular excitement for the upcoming trip. Leading up to my departure, there were some moments when I thought I just could not do it, but deep down in my soul I heard Jono's encouraging voice saying, 'C'mon, Mum, you can do this. You know I'll be with you.' I did feel his presence frequently, but sometimes I would question whether I was just imagining him. I do now believe that when I feel him it is so much more than my imagination, but I am also comforted knowing that anything that helps give meaning in a tormenting time is perfectly acceptable.

We live an hour and a half from the airport. As Perry drove me in, there were many thoughts racing through my mind. The memory of my last plane trip kept returning and I would shudder as I remembered how it felt on that long flight from New Zealand to Melbourne. I was trying hard to stop that feeling recurring. I kept reminding myself of the reward of this flight: seeing my beautiful daughter and her two daughters.

In my mind, I asked Jono to help me with two things on this flight:

1. Please arrange for whoever sits next to me to be someone who doesn't want to talk a lot.
2. Could that person also be someone who didn't cough a lot, and who fitted in their own seat without our bodies touching!

When I arrived at the airport, I was disappointed to be told an aisle seat was not possible. I repeated my requests to Jono but in my louder 'mind voice'! He did not disappoint me. After I was seated, a man around Jono's age took the seat beside me. He was on the aisle. He stowed his baggage in the overhead hutch, along with his jumper that he had taken off. It was with absolute delight that I was able to read what was printed within a circle on his t-shirt. It read EMPATH! And on the back, it read 'brotherhood of love'. After my first request to stretch my legs, followed by my apology for disturbing him, his response was, 'Please don't say sorry. Just let me know whenever you need to get out.'

I think the only conversation we had was when I commented how difficult it must be being an empath on a long-haul flight. We both laughed and didn't speak again, but I could feel the warmth of his soul. Jono had heard my request.

My three weeks with my UK family in Watford provided amazing respite and distraction. I discovered that even though my grief had not lessened, I now truly needed to 'dose' myself with how and when I revisited my grief. I had the charge of a four-year-old and an eight-year-old during most days, as my daughter worked from home. It was really what my soul

Chapter Six   Walking the traumatic grief path

needed. I was kept busy, entertained, loved, and basked in the wonderful warmth of England's summer. It was good to escape the depths and greyness of a Melbourne winter.

The third day I arrived in England was Jono's two-month anniversary of his death. I walked with my daughter to grab a coffee and then she returned to work. I said I would just wander up and down High Street, refamiliarising myself with this very English street. Sitting on the garden seat at the top of High Street, I could hear a busker in the distance. The songs she sang totally connected me to Jono, each one of them in different ways. I sat there drinking coffee, listening to her great songs, and I cried. After listening for about half an hour, I began walking to find where this voice was coming from. She had such a great amplification system that it was quite some time before I saw her. I waited for a gap in between songs, so I could drop my coins in her guitar case, and quickly said, 'Thank you for those beautiful songs. It's two months since my son died and all your songs were a great comfort.' She immediately unplugged her guitar and took my hand to say how sorry she was.

'How did he die?' she asked, and I explained he had taken his own life.

She said, 'I knew you were going to say that. My best friend took her own life six months ago, and I cried every day for the first few months.'

I could not speak, and she just hugged me and said, 'Just know there are people who love you, and it won't feel this bad forever.'

There were many brief encounters, such as this, that completely amazed me. It felt like Jono was offering me his love and comfort through many people, whether they were strangers or not.

For as many of these special casual encounters, there were some awkward moments as I reunited with UK friends and my daughter's extended family. It hadn't been long since Jono died and it still felt very raw. People, generally, did not feel comfortable speaking about his death, especially when they thought it might make me sad or make me cry. As hard as I tried, I could not disguise or prevent my tears. I just kept saying to people that crying is just what happens, but I asked them not to stop the conversation when it became difficult. I needed to keep saying his name. Of course, there were also many times when the subject was not Jono and that would bring light relief for many.

One of my planned activities with my granddaughters was to create a memory box for their Uncle Jono. While working in palliative care, I encouraged and assisted children, and sometimes adults too, in creating a special space where they could keep memories of their loved one who had died. They could visit the box whenever they wanted to feel close to their person.

My granddaughters and I chose things that would help them to connect with their Uncle Jono and prompt conversations about their memories of him. They chose from the many

Chapter Six Walking the traumatic grief path

photos I had brought with me which ones they wanted to paste on the lid. We had a fun day, talking about different times they had spent together. My four-year-old granddaughter had little memory of Uncle Jono, as it had been several years since she had seen him. She was only just turning two the last time they were together, but we enjoyed chatting about all the things Jono enjoyed doing with them.

There was one moment when I thought my heart might break in two. One space remained for a final photograph on the lid of the box and my four-year-old granddaughter said, 'This one has to go there.' She chose a photo of Jono holding his cat. She followed on by saying, 'He'll really like seeing that there, when he comes home.'

I looked at her and asked, 'Comes home?'

She answered, saying, 'He is coming home, isn't he?'

My honest response was, 'No, Uncle Jono will not come home.'

She was incredulous. 'What, never?'

I saw such sadness in her eyes as she tried to digest this idea.

'No, never,' I told her gently.

I explained that every time we think of him really hard, we might be able to feel him close to us. When it's a windy day, we can imagine there is a part of him in the wind. When we look at the stars at night, we can imagine that there's a part of him up there in that big space. At some level this soothed her, but my pain in watching her accept the truth that he would never come home triggered the same reminder to *me* that he would never come home.

I had learned about children's grief responses some years previously. This age group has difficulty accepting that death is permanent. According to their developmental age, they have magical thinking and find it difficult to understand the dead person will not come back to life. I was taken back to a memory from years ago. I spoke about this to my staff at the time, and reiterated the importance of using real words, rather than euphemisms such as 'passed away' or 'gone to sleep'. It was hard to convey to my granddaughter that Jono would not come home because part of me wanted to live in the magical world of believing he might. However, as we spent more time together, I confirmed that just because we would never see Uncle Jono again didn't mean we needed to stop talking about him.

My daughter was redesigning her back garden while I was in the UK so there were lighter moments, even resembling fun, when we purchased plants to be put in pots to line her fence-line. Then there was the job of painting her fences. This was a job that she had hoped Jono would have helped her with on his planned trip back in June. Having physical goals seemed to help so much, and even when it might be difficult to keep going with them, the sense of completion when the fence was done really did lift our spirits. Although my daughter did most of the painting, I helped too. We were not sure whether Jono would have done a better job than us, or whether the two of us had done better than he would have done. Either way, it somehow brought him closer to us, and completing the painting job was something the three of us could celebrate—Jono included.

The summer of 2022 was quite hot in the UK, and my daughter had a small swimming pool for the girls to cool down. It was big enough for all of us to get in and create some amazing fantastical adventures. After several weeks, the bottom of the pool started going green with algae, but as my daughter and I emptied it to clean it, we were both gobsmacked. There, in the bottom of the pool, was a very clear heart shape that was not green. It stood out as though Jono was sending his love directly to us.

My daughter's garden was looking lovely following our potting and painting efforts, and we spent many evenings sitting in the deck chairs, or on the daybed, with a glass or two of red: reminiscing, remembering, planning, crying and laughing. Sometimes, we just accepted the pure joy of being with each other, but then it was always tinged with the reality that we live so far apart. We filled every moment with something that made us happy. Together, we completed watching the whole series of 'Virgin River'! Now, there was a great distraction.

My time in the UK went very quickly, and before I knew it I was saying goodbye to my family and readying myself to return to Melbourne. While it is never pleasant saying goodbye, I was comforted by the knowledge that they would all return to Australia for Christmas. This would be our first Christmas without Jono.

I arrived at Heathrow Airport to commence my journey home, feeling quite a mess with many mixed emotions. I again attempted to get a seat near the aisle, or better still, with no one beside me. I remember my tearful explanation at the airline desk, as to why I would benefit from being alone. The airline staff member was very sympathetic and I wondered whether that was tears I saw in her eyes. Of course I understood the difficulties in granting my wish, especially when others had already had their seats allocated.

Sitting in the waiting area, I couldn't stop crying, but what I noticed was that it did not have the same traumatic feel about it. I felt just so sad, but I no longer felt as though I was on 'alert'. It felt a little like my internal alarm system had diminished. I was curious if this meant I was on my way to healing from trauma.

I decided that on my return to Australia, I would revisit that psychologist and start to explore the beginning of my grief.

Chapter Seven
It's all in the timing

In the previous chapters, I spoke about specific events or tasks that took place in the weeks following Jono's death. What follows now is how certain times and dates had a huge impact on me.

Living through the previous years of COVID-19 lockdowns, time had taken on a new perspective for many people. Losing track of the years or forgetting when previous events had occurred was something many of us had become familiar with.

When a traumatic death slams you in the face, time has almost no relevance. Days simply merge from one to the next. I had read amongst the myriad of literature that I thought might 'help' me, that returning to predictable routines is something to work toward. That sounded like good advice and one that in years gone by I had also offered grieving families. My problem was there was very little in my life that was predictable. Jono taking his own life was the most horrific and unpredictable event that could ever happen, so apart from the sun rising in the morning and setting in the evening, I had little faith in predictability. I could find little in routine that made any sense. I kept on reaching for a yesterday that always seemed to be just out of reach. I had no idea what tomorrow would bring.

Since my return from the UK, I had started visiting my psychologist every six weeks or so. I felt supported, understood, and free to express anything I wanted, anyhow I wanted to. This became something regular that I could rely upon. Perhaps this was the recommencement of a routine. I also knew that I felt so much more at ease after each visit. The psychologist was very empathetic, and I felt they were in some way walking this journey with me.

Five months to the day that Jono died, I found my anxiety increasing as the time of his death got closer. As 11:21 am approached, I felt an overwhelming urge to take a walk. I was drawn to one of the many walks in nature that I am fortunate enough to live close to. Even though it looked like it might rain, I walked very briskly to a safe place I knew amongst the trees—a place where I knew I would be on my own. Five minutes before the time Jono jumped in front of that train, it felt as though I was re-experiencing his pain. I began crying uncontrollably, but it was so much more than that. Suddenly, that familiar but almost unrecognisable sound of agonising deep pain within was escaping from what I think was my mouth, but I couldn't be sure. I was unable to focus on anything. I could feel my heartbeat rushing and I was even having difficulty breathing. I was totally unprepared for what happened next.

Chapter Seven It's all in the timing

At what I knew to be the exact time of his death, I seemed able to take a deep breath and slowly, but very definitely, my panic was replaced with peace. I still sobbed, but now it was a gentle cry. It somehow felt that Jono was now at peace. His pain and agony had subsided and therefore mine had too. I felt free from the pain and the panic I had previously been feeling. Perhaps this was also Jono's experience.

I had great difficulty in describing this to anyone, but as I reflected on that time it was as though I had been given a glimpse into the last moments of Jono's life. Apart from jumping onto the train tracks and my life coming to an end, I felt I had lived through some of the emotions that Jono may have gone through in the last moments of his life. It was as though I had surrendered to the unknown and the unpredictable. It left me shaken, but, strangely, filled with love. Was that Jono's arm I could feel around me? Had he allowed me a glimpse of his agony so I might attempt to understand his actions on that day? Did this release him from his pain?

It was now raining quite steadily, but it felt gentle to me. My walk back home felt cleansing as I was softly caressed by the rain. Unlike Jono, I had survived and was able to come back to my place of love.

As previously mentioned, apart from my regular visit to my psychologist, my routines had become irregular, and one day I realised a haircut was long overdue. When I rang my hairdresser (who, just by the way, I have been seeing for 40 years!) and explained my delay in booking a haircut, he very generously offered me the first available day and time. I gratefully accepted. When that day arrived, I awoke knowing I was not ready for that trip. My tears were too frequent, and I didn't feel able to go outside my front door. I rang my hairdresser, very apologetically, to re-schedule. He was very understanding and offered another date for the following week, which, again, I accepted. Yet, there was a nagging in the depths of my unknown, as I knew this would mean a train trip to the city.

It suddenly struck me the night before my haircut was due that the appointment I accepted meant I had to travel to the city on Jono's six-month anniversary. The time I had to catch the train for the 50-minute ride was around the time of Jono's death.

Until that point, I had brief moments of thinking I was becoming stronger, or perhaps I at least longed to become stronger. I tried to convince myself I could conquer any uncertainty I had about my first train trip. I thought by facing these challenges it might miraculously hasten my grief. I recall pleading with Jono to be present with me on that train trip.

As I walked down the train platform, I glanced at the large clock above me as it glaringly reminded me the time was 11:21 am. This was the time Jono died. I took several deep breaths as silent tears streamed down my face while I continued walking steadily down that platform. I consciously placed one foot in front of the other and had to remind myself to breathe. I could not allow myself to enter the space I had felt the previous month. I focussed on my deep breathing and calling in Jono's love to provide the strength to help get me on the train.

I turned my back to the train as I heard it approaching.

I could not bring myself to look at what Jono must have looked at six months previously. I only turned when the train stopped.

As I took my seat on the train, I envisioned Jono beside me. I imagined he was sitting on the seat next to me. In my mind, I continually asked him to let me feel his presence and take the ride with me.

I spoke to him in my mind, all the way into the city, and he offered comfort and chatter. I have an understanding that thoughts are the language of the brain and Jono and I exchanged our own language for the whole trip. I firmly believe there are many things that can't be explained by science or common sense, and sensing Jono's presence and his soothing love is something no one can take away from me. I have no need to 'prove' this because I feel it and know it as my truth. As I speak with others whose loved ones have died, I know this is not an unusual experience. I have taken comfort in and also offered comfort to those who describe similar experiences to me.

I had been a wedding celebrant for around twelve years when Jono died, and I was totally undecided as to whether I had the capacity to continue to do this after his death. When I commit to being the celebrant for a wedding, I give everything

I have and it often feels as if I am channelling the love of the couple. It demands a lot of me emotionally and I was uncertain whether I still had this within me. My internal tank was feeling empty. Through various 'coincidences', I came to accept that Jono was offering signs along the way that encouraged me to continue this part of my life.

My son, Jonathan Daniel Peck, was born on the 7th of June. I accepted the role of celebrant for two weddings, one month after the other. The name of the groom for the first wedding was Jonathan. He was such a wonderful groom with many gentle characteristics that reminded me so much of my own Jonathan. What a privilege to be Jonathan's (and his beautiful wife's) celebrant on one of the happiest days of his life. The name of the groom for the second wedding was Daniel and his birthday was 6th of June, the day before my Jonathan Daniel's birthday.

These details may appear to some as coincidental, or of little consequence, but I have a much stronger sense that it was Jono's way of encouraging me to do what he knew I loved doing. He wanted me to be the best celebrant I could.

Because I felt a lot of support from my 'special source', I successfully completed both weddings. They were very special and significant weddings to me. Once again, I felt my Jono's love shining through and coming directly into my soul.

For many months following Jono's death, it felt as if I had lost the organisational capacity I once had. Sometimes, things would simply be put into a cupboard to keep them out of

Chapter Seven It's all in the timing

sight. I always knew that when the time was right, I would go back to that cupboard and do a thorough sort through. As I said, time took on a new way of being, and even the time to tidy things, never really came.

This particular day I was looking for something I had not seen for months, but I had a strong feeling it must be in the linen cupboard. I began systematically removing the contents from each shelf, sorting through the items and placing them back neatly where they belonged. As I came to the top shelf, my heart seemed to skip a few beats.

There was the beautifully hand-woven green shawl Jono had been wrapped in as a baby.

It had been given as a gift by my sister upon Jono's birth. He always felt so soft and cuddly when I held him in that shawl. Suddenly, my mind had stepped back 32 years as I sobbed into the shawl, remembering my beautiful, much-loved baby. I had been keeping that shawl so I could pass it down to him for his own future babies. Not only was Jono no longer on this earth, but I had also been brutally reminded that I would never hold his own babies in my arms. He had told me, only months before, how much he had been looking forward to the day when he became a father. At that moment, not only did I feel my own sadness, but I swear I felt Jono's tears on my cheeks as well.

We were approaching Christmas, and I felt a familiar sense of dread of facing another 'first'. The excitement of seeing my daughter and her girls from the UK, as well as my older granddaughter joining us from Queensland, went some way to mitigate the dread of the occasion.

Jono loved Christmas and the only times we had not been together on Christmas Day during his lifetime was when one or the other of us was not in the same country. The joy and love of family coming together to celebrate, drink great wine and eat wonderful food was something our whole family shared. I could not imagine how I would get through this day without Jono's presence.

My delightful granddaughters contributed to the anticipation of our joint family love for this Christmas Day. The younger two helped decorate the Christmas tree and we created a beautiful decoration from a photo of Jono, which took pride of place on our tree.

When Christmas Day arrived, I busied myself with food preparation and tried as hard as I could not to focus on what we didn't have (Jono) but instead focus on what we did have: the love and people that were present.

As much as I wanted this to be a lovely day for all, I felt I failed at many levels. I mistakenly felt responsible for trying to understand how everyone else was feeling and focussed on making it 'better' for all present. Instead of taking one moment at a time, I felt I overcompensated by trying to ensure that everyone else was managing the day. There were times when I would try to imagine what might be coming and cut it short before it happened. I was trying to avoid any deep sadness on this day both for myself and others, which in retrospect meant

Chapter Seven *It's all in the timing*

I wasn't really being true to myself.

This, inadvertently, made it much worse for many. At the end of the day, as well as missing Jono beyond belief, I thought I had also damaged other relationships within the family. I really beat myself up and felt isolated from everyone. I had a strong feeling that I really needed to talk to Jono and even apologise to him, to say sorry that I had somehow stuffed up Christmas Day, as well as potentially some family relationships. But he was not there physically, so instead I spoke quietly to him in my mind. It did not bring peace, and I slept fitfully that night.

Despite my lack of sleep, I looked forward to a family day at the beach on Boxing Day. It was such a wonderful Aussie beach day, and we prepared our leftovers for a picnic lunch.

We set up a great spot and the others went off for a swim, seemingly filled with lots of laughter and lots of love. When they returned to our patch, it was my turn to swim in the sea.

As I slowly walked out into the ocean, I kept thinking how wonderful it would be to join Jono ... like right at that moment. I also kept pondering how I may have damaged family relationships the previous day and that really it would be better for everyone if I just wasn't here anymore. If I died today, I thought, nobody would have to be concerned or worried about me anymore and I would have a chance to be with Jono again.

I walked and walked straight ahead in the water and didn't turn back to the laughter and chatter I could hear from my family behind me on the beach. I just kept walking, focussed on wanting to walk to Jono. As previously stated earlier, this was not the first time I had encountered these thoughts since Jono died, but right now, on this day, it appeared that I had a means of joining him. It was in front of me. I kept walking out into the sea until my feet could no longer touch the bottom and I wanted to keep going. The pain I had inside felt too great for me to bear, and I struggled with the thought of not knowing if this was going to be the point of raising the white flag and saying, 'I give up'.

At the point of totally giving in to the sea and floating away forever, I felt a sudden surge of love coming from Jono. He was already with me, and I knew then his love would remain with me forever. He was telling me it wasn't my time yet. At that very moment, he forced me to consider how the family would possibly cope with another suicide. Did I really want to put them through more pain than they currently had?

I stopped my thoughts of no return as I felt Jono's presence. Instead, I just swam for what felt like forever. The water helped to melt the indescribable pain. The thoughts of leaving this earth hadn't absolutely abated; however, the suicide thoughts for that day had left me. The alternative thought to suicide was considering that I may be lucky enough to develop a terminal illness or dying a natural death. After all, I had already lived a very full nearly 67 years and I would have no regrets if my life came to an end.

I now accept the thoughts I had while walking into the sea

Chapter Seven It's all in the timing

that day as 'normal' and experienced by many who are deeply affected by grief. On that day I felt alone and hadn't fully realised this common thread runs through the lives of many bereaved mums. I also know that I was very lucky Jono was with me on that day as he didn't want me to die then. Weeks later, I was overcome with shame that I would even consider leaving this earth, but on Boxing Day it was very real.

A few days later, when I disclosed the thoughts I had on Boxing Day to some family members, I realised that I had totally overacted to Christmas Day. Probably the only person who felt family relationships were damaged was me. There had been no long-term damage that had arisen from my overthinking and overreacting to many things on Christmas Day. We were still able to be there for each other, and as I asked for forgiveness I was reassured there was nothing to forgive.

It took some time to release the thoughts of my imminent death and it left me searching even harder for a strong purpose where I might be able to contribute my broken self in a meaningful way. I needed an anchor. I was slowly becoming aware that grief is not the enemy, and, in many ways, it shows us the way to our future footsteps. The depths of my experienced grief gave me new insights, and although still not totally clear, to how I might be able to turn the experience of Jono's death into something helpful for others. Even if it was just that I might validate such an unthinkable experience for others, then that would be a way of honouring my grief experience.

A new year had soon begun, but I could not find it within me to wish anyone a Happy New Year. I wondered how I would ever find myself back to any 'happy' place ever again.

I was fortunate enough to officiate at a wedding on New Year's Eve and it felt like a beautiful gift because it happened to be in a little country town. Perry and I decided we would stay the night. It removed the pressure and expectation that New Year's Eve brings, and we would not be surrounded by familiar things.

Again, as I began the wedding ceremony, I found myself stepping into the beautiful circle of love shared by two. The contagious feeling of a loving couple coming together, surrounded by family and friends, is such a bonus for a celebrant. This began a gentle entrance into a year ahead where I committed to start exploring new ways of living without such indwelling deep sadness.

I recognised there was something very different about me since Jono died, and probably would be for the rest of my life. His absence was everywhere I looked. Without sounding melodramatic, I had to relearn how to be in this world without him. I was a bereaved mother whose youngest, much-loved son had died. I still had difficulty saying that out loud. I had loved and nurtured him and had always been there for him, except, as it now appeared, when he needed me the most. This was the new me that I had to reshape. I knew I would never be my old self again and—somehow—I had to learn how to grow into my new self. A part of me recognised that this new me would develop and grow from the very depths of my grief.

Chapter Seven   It's all in the timing

The next few months were rather gentle, and Perry and I started to participate in activities that were familiar. We went and stayed in Clunes (a beautiful small country town in Victoria) to attend the close-by Newstead Live Folk Festival. We shared the weekend with some special friends, the sort of friends who understood the unexpected tears that still erupted from nowhere.

The following month we had tickets to see one of my favourite singers, Sting. So, off we went to stay at Torquay (a beautiful coastal town in Victoria). We went to a winery where the concert was held to enjoy a great night. That was the first time I found myself singing out loud and even had the energy for dancing. For a flicker of a moment, I was able to put aside my sadness. Later, I felt slightly guilty for this spurt of joy, but I was quite relieved when my psychologist told me this is a common response during the grieving journey. I needed to learn to give myself permission to tap into the joy that had been absent in my life since Jono's death.

I wondered if I had begun what is commonly referred to as the 'healing journey'. There were moments I was convinced that I would never 'heal'; in fact, I wasn't even sure what that meant. A part of me was even a little afraid as I wondered if I might distance myself from Jono if I 'healed'. There was one part of me that did not want anyone to take away my grief as I thought that might take away my closeness to Jono. I always wanted to follow the lead of my sadness and I hoped it would lead me to a safer soul destination. It often felt I was experiencing something for the first time when offered a glimpse of enjoyment. Somehow, all life experiences felt different and took on a different perspective since Jono's death. I had read—in one of those textbooks from previous years—that this is referred to 'relearning your new world'. Perhaps, after all, there had been some words of wisdom in those books. I discuss this further in a later chapter.

As many of us already know, whatever grief experience we are living with we quickly learn it is not linear. It doesn't have a trajectory which slowly lessens the pain. Suddenly, one morning in March, nine months after Jono died, I woke up with overwhelming heaviness and could not stop crying.

What was going on? It had already been nine months, so why were my mind and body responding in ways that felt like it was during the first few days after his death? I cancelled everything that was in my diary for the week ahead and planned to just bunker down and take as long as I needed. I did not want to face the world. Again. I really felt in a mess. I wanted to cocoon myself, rolling up in a small ball in warm blankets. I wondered if this is what is referred to as being 'paralysed' by my messy grief. There were many phrases I had heard in the past, and when it came to my next new experiences, those familiar words came flooding to me in ways that now made sense. I have never been able to separate myself from my soul, so I knew it had something to say to me and I needed to hear it. To do that, I needed to be still.

Chapter Seven It's all in the timing

In my mind I had begun to feel the weight of my grief diminishing a little in my life, and as I referred to it previously, grief had almost become my friend. But now it felt like it had run ahead of me, increased in size and hid behind a rock. As I walked past that rock, it jumped out unexpectedly and tried to overpower me. I was ambushed by grief.

I was overwhelmed all over again with the deep sadness and reality I would never see Jono again on this earth. I was having flashbacks to the night I received the phone call from Tony telling me that Jono had killed himself. I buried my head in Jono's unwashed t-shirts, trying desperately to still smell some of his scent that may have remained. I panicked when it felt like I might even be losing some of my memories of Jono, and I could hardly believe I could never return to the world where Jono was alive. I wasn't sure how I would get back to the place I had been only weeks before.

We live on a hill not far from a railway station. Every time the train pulls into the station, it blows its whistle and that noise floats up right to our house. After reading the statement to the police from the train driver, where he claimed to have blown his whistle for a solid seven seconds before Jono jumped, the noise of the train whistle began to haunt me. I tried as hard as I could not to hear it by simply ignoring it, but I couldn't, and every time I heard it I revisited the moments before Jono jumped onto the tracks.

During this time, when I felt ambushed, the noise from the train whistle became almost unbearable. It was a constant reminder of those moments before Jono jumped to his death. In my distress I reached the conclusion that we would have to relocate—and I really love where we live—or I was going to have to do some serious work on myself.

As I snuggled up in my cocoon, I tried my hardest to escape from the world for what turned out to be a week. In desperation to free myself from this all too familiar pain, I chose to do some serious 'grief work'. I had an abundance of grief resources, which I had shared with so many others over the years, so I thought it was time for me to start relooking through the plethora of books and articles.

I came across an exercise for those who had not been given an opportunity to say goodbye or where your person had died unexpectedly. The exercise suggested writing them a letter of all the things you would have liked to have said to them before they died. I spent the afternoon focussing my attention on what I would want to say to Jono. I tried to imagine that his time on this earth had simply expired and he was preparing to leave. I tried to believe his life had been completed. I envisaged that my loving ancestors were on their way to collect him and take him to the next dimension. I imagined he was on his way to that next place, wherever that was. I removed all the trauma from my thoughts and told him in my letter all the wonderful things about him that I wanted him to know. There was so much I was proud of and many loving, funny memories. I then imagined handing this letter to him on that railway platform and him reading it and embracing me. In my mind, he wished me farewell, promising his love would always remain with me, and then he left in the arms of our very special ancestors. The whistle of the train transformed into a triumphant farewell, rather than a traumatic warning.

Almost instantly, the noise I continued to hear from the passing trains offered me a message of love. It reminded me of the promise he made, that his love will remain with me forever. If we focus hard enough, our minds can reframe many experiences, and I was now rid of the trauma of those train whistles. It took several days of feeling the warmth of the sun's rays, sleeping when I needed, practicing some breath exercises, spending time writing, having a few hot baths, and sitting in the memory (or was it the spirit?) of Jono. I knew he would not want my grief to disable me and during this time I imagined I could even feel his arms around me as I wept. In whatever way I chose to give meaning to all my experiences, it worked for me. It may not be the same for everyone, but my way of meaning-making provided me with comfort.

Some of my close friends became aware that I had hit a rough patch and I was trying to endure a difficult time. Declining their visits or coffee catchups, and even declining phone calls, was a sure sign for them that times were tough. I also think they understood this tricky time would be limited. They had come to accept that some things we must complete on our own.

As the days wore on, I slowly felt as though I was gently

breaking out of my cocoon and ever so gradually coming back into the world. I cautiously began stretching each limb as I broke out from what had been sheltering me.

I was very aware, as I rejoined my community of loving people around me, that it may not be the last time this happens, but it also might be different every time.

I knew instinctively that I must be prepared for the hard slog, the sad moments, the joyous moments, the frustrating moments, and all the parts in between. I know that on some days I experience all the above, while other days just become other days.

The moments and times I have written about are significant memories. There are many more tough moments in between that I scoot around daily. I guess I always will.

Chapter Eight
The golden rule

I have told my story. I have attempted to explain aspects of my experience following the death of my son. It feels as though I have bared my soul as I display my emotional and spiritual self to all.

In the following chapters I hope to offer more of my teaching self. I will now draw from my thoughts and attempt to make cognitive sense. The next part of this book still relies on my own experiences, but I am hoping it will be useful for people who wish to support bereaved parents in the best possible way.

Speaking with someone recently, I was really surprised to learn that they had reached adulthood without experiencing a significant death of someone close. As I have been surrounded by death, either personally or professionally for most of my life, I tend to forget that death is not as familiar to others as it is to me. Even as I write this, I have lived through the deaths of another three family members since Jono's death. I would like death to take a holiday right now, but I know that it may not.

I have previously said that Jono's death was so incomparable to anything at all familiar and was like no other death experience I had. It remains that way. Even if I had thought that death and dying was the area I could offer myself, when Jono died I just wanted to say, 'please stop now. I don't want to be in this space anymore'.

For those who are reading about death and have not experienced a close death, I offer you compassion, and heartfelt understanding for what you will most certainly face one day.

I firmly believe that we still exist within a 'death denying' society. Before Jono's death, I would facilitate frequent community workshops encouraging people to complete advance care planning. Completing documents was not my main focus—it was discussing death. We spent a lot of creative time coming up with substitute words for death and sometimes, within my presentations, I can fill a whiteboard full of people's suggestions for the replacement word/s of 'dead'. No one will get out of this life alive, and yet we still do not wish to discuss or plan our own death. Sometimes I wonder if people think they might die sooner if they start talking about it. It is still a subject a lot of people are afraid of. I heard someone on the radio last week say, 'Talking about pregnancy won't make you pregnant, just like talking about dying won't kill you.' Not so many generations ago, we did death naturally. We now appeared to have handed it over to professionals so they 'take it out of our need to worry about it'.

Let's start the discussion within book clubs, or meeting up for coffee, or gathering as we share meals together. If we can't even talk about death, how do we expect to respond appropriately to grief, let alone suicide?

Chapter Eight The golden rule

As a society, we are not taught about the emotional aspect of reacting or responding to death. Strangely, we see death on our screens every single day. It may be natural disasters, crime related deaths, motor vehicle accidents, wars, terrorism, or the deaths of well-known celebrities. We are exposed to death daily, but we are not offered any education or support on how to respond when it is someone we love or care about. We are certainly not educated in how to support others who experience the death of a family member within their lives. Unless we reach out to the 'specialised field' we are not given any tools to support people in their grief. I wonder if communication, along with empathy and active listening, was taught in schools whether our society may be in a better position to respond to our grieving community. Instead, we rely on the many clinicians who research the area of grief and provide some brilliant academic results. I would say this is the other end of the spectrum.

I remember when I learned to play the piano, I was told to spend as much time on the theory as I did on the practical. I now reflect on how that theory sometimes got in the way of my freedom to play exactly as I wanted to. It seemed to somehow restrict my movement because I was trying to comply with the written material I had studied. It was drummed into me how important it was to have the theoretical knowledge. I understand now that I was being taught to read the building blocks of music, but I also know many people who never 'learnt' the theories of piano playing yet play with such brilliance. Sometimes, I see the same analogy with grief theories.

Having worked and studied grief, death and dying for more than 25 years, I have become familiar with a broad range of theory. There is copious amounts of research and study, and some incredible academics have put many years into producing some great research.

Please don't think that I don't have high regard for these academics, or that I am trying to diminish any of these specialists' findings. There are many theories, as I will discuss in the next chapter, that are brilliant and make perfect sense. I have become aware of how some of these theories have applied to my own grief journey. However, there also seems to be some very outdated or restrictive beliefs regarding grieving individuals and the journey they travel. Listening to the lived experience can be very beneficial alongside the theory.

Listening is everything.

If you have chosen to read this book because you know someone whose child has died by suicide, and you are not sure what to say to that person, the chapter discussing the power of language may offer guidance, particularly in what not to say. Most grieving people are so distressed in the early days that they don't always even hear what people say to them, but I can absolutely confirm how upsetting it is to receive some 'advice', or worse still, an untrue statement from someone who thinks they know better. There is a certain vulnerability in those early days of grieving that requires gentleness and compassion. It does not include what the friend/neighbour/church friend/relative thinks the bereaved person should be told. Mostly, the best response any grieving person can receive is for someone just to *listen* and not to be afraid to weave the name of the person who has died into their conversation. That can feel like gold.

This is what I mean about the lived experience accounts needing to sit alongside the theory. Sometimes, just the small and simple things are so much more appreciated, like listening.

When someone dies, particularly if it's an unexpected death, or if they have taken their own life, those that loved them need to continue to tell their story. Each time they tell the story, even if it is through their tears, it is cathartic. There are many things to remember about a life that appears to end much sooner than it should. There are many things to talk about.

The golden rule: become a compassionate listener. Be curious about the person who has died. Hear the pain of the bereaved without judgement. Don't provide advice or ever think you 'know better' than those who are trying to survive their own grief. It is their experience.

Chapter Nine
Putting the focus on theories

I began to learn about the many theories of grief as I researched and wrote the 'Lived Experience of Grief' for my Social Work (Hns) degree. Specialists in the field at the time were highly respected and they wrote many books and publications which enhanced the practice of many grief practitioners. I hold them in high respect. I did find it interesting though, that the majority of research was based on research projects with white, mainly middle-aged bereaved women. I believe this has since been extended beyond this cohort; however, what I learnt back then felt somewhat limited. Some of what I learned at the time helped make sense of my previous bereavement experiences, which until that time had been reasonably limited.

I reflect now, how strange it is that what we learn from written knowledge we find so easy to apply with a broad stroke to most general situations. I am sure there are grief counsellors who draw from many theories I discovered, in turn providing great support to bereaved people.

Without any disrespect to all those people who offer professional support to the bereaved, I wish to encourage them to know those theories well, but to please look beyond the existing models and truly engage with a soul connection to the bereaved person. I believe we should be encouraged to learn to live with our grief, rather than be offered a medical or pathological response to help 'get over it'.

Stages of grief

I am still astonished when I search for the word 'grief' on the internet to see how many articles still refer to 'stages of grief'. The well-known and much publicised five stages of grief include: denial; anger; bargaining; depression and acceptance. I am not suggesting that we don't feel these things throughout our grief, but it is not possible to package these emotions into stages or provide timeframes. Such emotions are not able to be boxed or contained to an aspect of grief, as not everyone feels them all, and certainly not in a linear fashion. The word 'stages' indicates that we move from one emotion to the other until we have completed the full circle, and then—miraculously—you have completed grieving. Grief is messy and tangled and does not come into our lives in neat packages. It continues in various ways throughout our lives.

Most people have heard of the originator of this theory, Elisabeth Kübler-Ross, the Swiss American psychiatrist, who is described as a pioneer in near death studies. Her work was brilliant, and she gave permission for everyone to start talking about death and dying. In fact, she encouraged this. After working extensively with dying patients, she claimed that in observing the dying, they appeared to experience five stages of emotions, as mentioned above. Subsequently, those theories were gradually transferred into grief during bereavement, and hence many people mistakenly promoted them as stages of grief following the death of a loved one. They initially were intended for dying people. Not for grief.

I was very intrigued with an entry that popped up in my online search: 'Free Online Grief Course – 4 Steps to Heal from Grief'. While I really hope this may provide help for some people, what needs to be remembered is that each person, and each grief experience, is so unique. I fail to imagine a good outcome with such a promotion. I almost laughed because wow! In only four steps I can be *healed*. It was obvious the person who had written this course had not experienced the grief of a child's death by suicide. The healing journey is not returning to life as it was before, but rather not allowing grief to damage or continually control your life. Someone once told me there is no quick way to get *over* grief, we must instead take it by the horns and feel every element of it as we go *through* grief. We cannot outwit grief, so we must find a way of sitting and having a relationship with it. I can confirm there is no quick route. I would have taken it if there was.

I recall many years ago as I facilitated a bereavement group for recently bereaved partners, one person admitting, 'I think there might be something wrong with me, because I haven't reached the "angry" stage of grief yet. I am just sad.' I remember trying to explain and dispel all the myths around

Chapter Nine Putting the focus on theories

the 'stages' model. It seemed that such an approach had become a prescription for grief, rather than a description.

Since Jono died, I have not experienced the emotions referred to within the 'stages' model in a linear fashion. That is not to say that some of the emotions mentioned haven't been present, but they have never been in any particular order. Sometimes I experience aspects of these emotions all in one day. I also know some days my grief is very raw. Other days it is not and then a few weeks or months down the track, it sneaks up behind me and tries to overwhelm me. I have previously referred to this feeling like an unexpected ambush. Grief does not provide a linear experience. How neat and tidy that would be.

I believe I have three personal stages of grief: the beginning, the middle, and the rest of my life. I don't believe I will continue to experience the great pain I feel today for the rest of my life ... well, at least I hope not. But what I do know is there will always be a hole in my heart that feels so large some days, and on other days I am able to hold it closer and it somehow reduces. As I heard someone say recently, 'the hole doesn't disappear, it will always be there, however, life grows around it'. That makes sense to me.

So, if you are working with a bereaved person, please accept that the 'stages' of grief are not the most helpful tool to explore what is happening to them as their soul continues to yearn for their loved one. They will probably miss that person for their remaining life.

The Dual Process

Back in 1999, two grief researchers, Margaret Stroebe and Henk Schutt, proposed a new way of looking at grief. Instead of promoting 'stages' of grief, they presented a way of moving in and out of the grief journey and referred to it as the 'dual process'.[2]

I know in the early days following Jono's death, I could never imagine myself moving away from feeling anything except the very depths of my loss. I could not anticipate any 'recovery'. I felt the loss so deeply that any suggestion of 'restoration' could easily have been a foreign language.

I do recall a day, about six weeks after Jono died, when I was required to 'dose' my grief, or in other words, to put it aside for a while. I was booked for my first wedding as a celebrant following Jono's death and I needed to focus on the love of the beautiful couple in front of me. This was their day and I had promised them and myself I would create the space and love they deserved. That is when I had my first experience of 'dosing' myself. I knew I would revisit my grief following the completion of their ceremony. As an aside, I did an amazing job as celebrant for the gorgeous couple and even joined them for a meal following their ceremony. I felt exhausted at the end of that day, but I had taken my first peek into a practice that I considered might be helpful in enabling me to continue dealing with my grief. I had been able to put it aside for a short time, knowing I could return to it later.

This is how the dual process works. It looks at two stressors experienced during grief. One being our loss and the other our restoration back to the everyday tasks of living. These two stressors criss-cross from one to the other, or using another descriptor, they oscillate. Time can be spent confronting grief and for me, that was the everyday realisation that Jono was not coming back; or it can be spent avoiding pain, which, from time to time, provides respite from loss. This respite enabled me to complete the everyday tasks that were still required in my life.

Earlier in the book, I talked about attending a Sting concert seven months after Jono died. It was the first time I felt able to sing out loud and dance. Without fully understanding what I was doing, I was giving myself permission not to feel sad for that evening. It was okay to enjoy some aspects of life. This did not mean I was 'over' my grief. I was taking a break from it.

I knew that I would be confronted by my loss forever, in varying degrees, but just for that one night I took respite from it. I imagined that I felt Jono there beside me, pleased to see me enjoying myself.

People offering support to those in grief need to accept that as bereaved people work toward grief becoming less agonising and debilitating, they also need to acknowledge that dark times are part of a lifetime journey. I recognise I will never fully 'get over' Jono being absent in my life, but I know that sometimes I am able to 'dose' myself with grief and leave it behind me as I take respite from it. Support people, and others, sometimes mistakenly view this respite as 'moving on' or 'recovery' from grief. I know it can appear to many as gaining strength, especially when I work hard at being the best celebrant I can be. What people don't witness is how I might cry all the way home following that ceremony. It is hard work learning to restore life following the death of your child, and the notion of zig-zagging in and out of loss and restoration is a good image. Encouragement from support people to do a little zig-zagging with grief may help lighten the load of the bereaved, without a mistaken belief that the bereaved has 'moved on'.

Relearning the world

Around 1996, a professor of philosophy, Thomas Attig, coined the phrase 'relearning the world' to describe the experience of life after someone you love dies. This theory acknowledges that following a significant death, the world is changed forever for the bereaved. After such a death, the bereaved must rebuild connections in new ways to anchor themselves to this world. He continues to encourage bereaved people to move from *being* our pain to *having* our pain.[3]

I have already described a little of the way I had to relearn this world without Jono being in it. I recall telling a friend I did not want my status of a grieving mother to define who I was. In part, this is what Attig is referring to when he said *being* our pain. I did not want to be so preoccupied with my loss that I cannot let anything else in.

Understand that even though bereaved parents will carry a variation of sadness for their child's death with them in their heart forever, there is still the capacity to hang on to hope. If the term 'hope' is used in any therapy, may it be to refer to a future for the bereaved where meaning can be given to their suffering.

Attig also suggests that people pay attention to the internal resilience they have. Some people have more than others, and as I have said previously, I frequently wonder whether resilience is something we are born with, or something that can be learned. I often wonder how people with less resilience than what I believe I was born with and developed during my life manage the journey of such tragic events. I am aware that some don't. Again, I encourage any grief support people to understand that relearning a new world without your child is a lifetime task. Harsh reminders lay along the way, sometimes making the new world look as though it is covered in an unreachable fog.

Continuing Bonds

Around 1996, grief researchers Dennis Klass, Phyllis Silverman and Steven Nickman started a revolution in the grief field called 'continuing bonds'. The first realisation these professionals came to was that death ended a life, but it did not necessarily end a relationship. They edited a book with 22 authors who contributed to this idea.[4] Thankfully, these days, this is a well-accepted concept and quite the opposite to the previously held belief that one had to 'let go' and 'move on'. There are many ways bereaved people are now encouraged to engage in an ongoing relationship with their person who has died.

I often consider my current relationship with Jono and how it compares to the relationship with my family in New Zealand. As I write this, I haven't seen Jono now for 25 months, but he remains in my thoughts daily. I haven't seen a lot of my family in New Zealand for much longer than this, but it doesn't mean I have stopped loving them or don't have a relationship with them.

Continuing bonds describes various ways of staying connected to your person beyond their death, including talking to the dead, sharing their stories, visiting their favourite place, celebrating their special days, and writing messages for them, which is something seen more recently on social media.

I have used many examples in this book to describe how I continue my relationship with Jono. My heart continues to search for any connection with him, and in this way I continue his legacy. This may change over time, but it will always be evolving, and I will never want to 'disconnect' from Jono. I will wear his socks until they have so many holes that they are no longer able to be worn! I will always be on the search for ways he may try to communicate or connect with me.

My hope is that any therapeutic or support people will encourage this ongoing relationship when they work alongside the bereaved. How this is done in a comfortable and meaningful way will be unique for every single person. Permission and encouragement from support people may ease any pressure from well-wishers to disconnect from the deceased.

Chapter Nine   Putting the focus on theories

Grief is like a storm at sea

Many years ago, I remember hearing an analogy of grief being like riding in a boat through a turbulent storm. If I remember it correctly, the **waves of emotion** referred to the many deeply felt emotions such as hopelessness, guilt, sadness, yearning, resentment, anger and despair. After Jono died, I could so easily relate to the description of these waves lapping at the side of the boat. Sometimes I even felt them coming inside the boat and I had moments wondering whether the boat would capsize.

That same boat then experienced the **winds of behaviour** which brought with them sleep disturbance, appetite disturbance, lack of concentration, restlessness, agitation and social withdrawal.

The boat was also affected by the **fog of thoughts.** These were thoughts that were full of confusion, feeling scared, being forgetful, being disorganised, thinking I was going crazy, and feeling out of control. There were some days when I remember experiencing these **emotions** and **behaviour** and **thoughts** all at once. It felt like the most turbulent storm of my life. I am also aware that the grief storm, like any other storm, can return at any time, sometimes totally unannounced.

The boat stayed afloat during the storm, but it incurred some damage. Even though the sails may have ripped, they were repaired, and as it started taking water in through the holes, the sides were patched. It was still the same boat, but it looked different and would never be in the same state as the original boat. As part of this image, I also remember being told of the vision of a distant lighthouse. Somehow, that lighthouse kept that little boat from smashing onto the rocks and being totally destroyed. I've held on to the image of the lighthouse and even though some days it appears far, far away, I know it is always there.

Fully understanding the impact of emotions, behaviours and thoughts during a grief storm may assist the bereaved to locate the lighthouse that will keep them from total destruction. Sometimes stormy weather continues intermittently, sometimes for a lifetime, and we need never lose sight of that lighthouse.

Complicated or prolonged bereavement

Now we come to a discussion that can make me a little upset, and an idea I find it difficult to grasp. By now, you might understand my belief that grief is really about learning to live life in a different way, because Jono, and the person you love, is not physically returning to this earth.

Within the medical model it seems that grief is now being pathologised as an illness.

The term 'complicated grief' has more recently been merged into the term 'prolonged grief'. Both phrases are commonly used to describe grief that is more intense or lasts longer than a culture may consider typical. It may also be described as an 'ongoing heightened state of mourning' that prevents healing and interrupts day-to-day life.

As I read about this type of grief, I feel a certain shame that perhaps I still experience parts of what I have just written. I find it interesting that it appears so easy for people working within this field to develop a criterion that sometimes appears full of judgement towards grief. It is as though they somehow know more about living with grief than the person who is surviving it.

There are some researchers who have created a convincing case that prolonged grief is a disorder, rather than a grieving process. I have already alluded to the fact that instead of grief being a process I believe it is a state of being.

What I have discovered in my recent research on this subject is that prolonged grief disorder (PGD) has been accepted globally. The World Health Organization publish 'International Classification of Diseases' (ICD), yes, you did read that correctly—it refers to 'diseases', and PGD has been included in the most recent publication in January 2022. In March 2022, 'prolonged grief disorder' was added to the Diagnostical and Statistical Manual of Mental Disorders (DSM). It now has a place in the DSM-5-TR.

What surprises me even more is that recent German research (Feb 2024) by Julia Treml, Katja Linde, Elmar Brahler, and Anette Kersting highlighted that even though both classification systems use the same name, the criteria content and diagnostic approach are different.[5]

The implication of this difference means that the prevalence of PGD will not be able to be affectively known, not even by professionals.

While I accept that clinically a PGD diagnosis may be of

great assistance to grief providers, and while I acknowledge that it may bring relief to some bereaved people, I will always feel cautious in having grief diagnosed as a mental disorder or a disease.

I know from previous experience as a grief counsellor that if clients described ongoing deep grief after six months, as professional support people, we would explore some aspects more deeply and then consider suggesting medical support, if this felt right for our clients.

I remember a visit to my psychologist around six months after Jono's death. I was so concerned that I might be encouraged to seek medical intervention. I was fearful of being 'diagnosed' with complicated grief, as it had now been six months and I was still sad and upset. Having heard my story from the beginning the psychologist looked at me and asked, 'And what part of your bereavement do you consider not to be complicated?'

I laughed with relief, knowing that they understood and in one sense normalised what I was experiencing. I have always felt validated during these sessions. I must emphasise that I am not discouraging medical intervention and medication if it is needed. For me, medicine cannot cure a broken heart, but a soul connection, whether it is professional or family or friend, provides a soothing balm. If I ran the world, I would prefer to focus on 'building up' the *village* so individuals experiencing deep grief are supported and loved by those who surround them. So many people who are grieving feel isolated, and I believe it would be far better to be loved and included within your community than to seek 'treatment' from a health provider.

I did find it rather humorous to read one article with the following interpretation of what causes complicated grief. 'It is not known what causes complicated grief.' (Really? What about the unexpected death of someone you love dearly. That might be a hint!) It continued, 'As with many mental health disorders, it may involve your environment, your personality, inherited traits and your body's natural chemical make-up.'

I began to think about what is considered normal grief. Does such a thing exist? Years ago, I recall telling newly bereaved clients that their grief experience was as unique to them as their fingerprint. Each of us are wonderful humans with unique characteristics and traits. We each grieve differently. This can also be the time for those closest to you, to acknowledge the pain of grief is not something easily 'fixed' or 'completed'.

I do not dismiss the reality that there may be people who are so preoccupied with the death of their person and their feeling of loss that it prevents them from participating in all life activities. There is a general agreement within research that approximately 10% of bereaved people experience what is now listed in the DSM as prolonged grief disorder. But as I previously stated, this percentage may increase if the criteria from ICD-11 is applied.

I don't necessarily believe one has to have experienced grief specific to a death to provide support or counsel. There are many wonderful professionals in the world who share a very deep understanding of the effects of grief, but I now know that my own experience has provided such deep insight that I would not have otherwise had. I know, since Jono's death, when I speak with other mums whose children have died that I truly understand their words. If you are someone who provides grief support, please always be open to learning from the bereaved people you support. Listen to their soul stories.

Sadness and a deep-seated loss over the unexpected suicide of my son will always be with me. I'm sure it is because I was so closely connected to Jono, but I hear him encouraging me to continue to do the many things in life that give me joy. My grief is so deep because my love for him was so strong.

There are many theories that support cultural norms, but let us never forget that people are people and labels are labels. My plea to all those professionals who offer grief support is to fully understand the many grief theories—then cast them aside, as you support each individual and different bereaved soul. In the words of Carl Jung, 'Know all the theories, and master all the techniques, but as you touch a human soul, be just another human soul ...'

My plea to all others who may find themselves in the company of bereaved mothers—in any aspect of community or as part of their village, especially if their children have taken their own life—is to check your language before trying to be 'helpful', and remember the golden rule: become a compassionate listener.

Chapter Ten
The power of language

It is not unusual for people to struggle with what to say to a newly bereaved parent, particularly to a suicide bereaved parent. I have noticed since Jono's death that if I disclose I am a bereaved parent, and extend that to saying 'he killed himself', the response becomes much more awkward. There really are no easy words, but please know that a hug or a touch on the arm is very comforting. Nearly everyone who has spoken to me has had the very best of intentions, despite their words not always being well crafted or sometimes, what I thought of as less heartfelt. The simplest but most comforting words I heard were, 'I'm so devastated for you. I don't know what to say except I love you, and I'm here for you. Tell me more about your son.'

Let me share with you some language, phrases and comments that upset me so much at the time that I often couldn't respond. Alongside them were other words that comforted and supported me. Please remember that every single person is unique and different, so my comfort and discomfort may not be the same for other bereaved parents. The way I hear words may not be the same for others. We all interpret language differently. I am only speaking of my response.

Number one

If I can get one point across to everyone about the language **NOT** to use when someone takes their own life, it is using the expression: 'committed suicide'. I have always found this very offensive and stigmatising, as it has connotations of committing a crime, and even though not everyone realises it, it is morally judgmental. This saying came about when suicide was a crime. Yes, a crime. Historically, people could be prosecuted or excommunicated from the church if they survived, as any attempt to take one's own life was seen as a sin.

In the state of Victoria, Australia, it was the *Crimes Act 1958 (Sect 6A)* that dismissed suicide as a crime. *'The rule of law whereby it is a crime for a person to commit or to attempt to commit suicide is hereby abrogated.'*

We have become accustomed to hearing the term 'committed suicide' with very few people understanding its origins. I suggest that the phrase is a relic from past legal codes and such wording perpetuates the stigma and moralistic attitude toward suicide.

Perhaps the reason that such judgemental language continues is not because people intend it to be harmful, but because most people do not understand why it shouldn't be used. Behind this is the taboo of having any discussion around suicide within the community or society generally, as it does not usually sit comfortably with people. It should be remembered that suicide is not a condition—it is a cause of death.

I suspect one of the reasons we don't discuss death by

suicide openly is because most people are afraid there may be copycat deaths. We are all familiar with news items that inform us of a death—usually a celebrity—followed by a statement like, 'there are no suspicious circumstances'. This is often followed by a list of helplines, which suggests the person had taken their own life.

What seems to be lacking in the suicide prevention space are specific tools.

At Jono's funeral, it was openly spoken that Jono had taken his own life. By his family and the funeral director (with our permission). At that time, I was aware there were some people present who were emotionally vulnerable and were devastated at Jono's death. Although I felt consumed with my own grief, I did not want any other parent to experience what we had been through as a family. Again, I did my own research to find some useful tools, and came across an incredible little book called *Just One Reason*. This is a mental health toolkit and offers simple techniques against suicidal thoughts. I bought several of these books and sent them off to those I thought might benefit from them.

I feel strongly we need to have public conversations about suicide, calling it for what it is, and offering a large array of responses, both within the mental health area and beyond. Families need to have these discussions with each other, so they can all find 'just one reason' to stay here.

Language can be stigmatising, but there are other words to describe suicide that are still clear.[6]

Stigmatising terminology	Appropriate terminology
Committed suicide	Died by suicide
Successful suicide	Suicided
Completed suicide	Ended his/her life
	Took his/her life
Failed attempt at suicide	Non-fatal attempt at suicide
Unsuccessful suicide	Attempt to end his/her life

In the early days after Jono's death, I did not have the strength to attempt to educate people, but it always took my breath away when people spoke of others they knew or had heard about who had 'committed suicide'.

Please train your brain to use the correct phrases such as: died by suicide; took his own life or killed himself. This explains exactly what happened without moral judgement and, strange as it may sound, I was relieved when people used those words when they talked about Jono's death.

Number two

Another mistaken presumption about suicide is that the person who died had a mental health history or had been suffering from depression. This book is not written with a focus on mental health. It is interesting to note, however, that even with more than 3000 Australians taking their own life every year, that is eight people every day, there is still no way of predicting who might be at higher risk of ending their own life.

Chapter Ten   The power of language

In fact, this comes from one systematic review:
95% of those who are designated as high-risk do not die by suicide, and 50% of those who do die by suicide come from the group which would be classified as low risk.[7]

Without doubt, some mental disorders do contribute to people ending their own life, but I believe we need to consider a wider range of cultural, economic, educational, family, and social circumstances. If such awareness was fully understood, suicide may sit well outside the resources of medicine and may then be more appropriately classified as a community problem.

The conclusion I am left with, as to why Jono chose to take his life on that day, was his response to a predicament he found himself in at that moment and felt no escape from. A moment of total overwhelm. I may never know what triggered that, but I also feel it was an immediate, unmeditated response, not given much time for thought. There are some in our family who strongly believe it was a 'mistake', but one too late to retreat from. I will never know for sure, but I can swear that sometimes I hear Jono telling me that his brain just 'frizzed' at that moment, or as I told the judge at the funeral, he had a glitch.

I still become upset when people insist on telling me that Jono must have been *suffering from depression*. It feels like they know a secret that should have been obvious to me. Jono was not depressed, and I do not enjoy the need to correct this assumption. To others this may sound quite trivial, but from a bereaved mother's perspective, using incorrect language or creating assumptions, or even using language with little thought of consequences, can be deeply hurtful.

Number three

'At least' – *he had fitted in a lot in his lifetime.*
'At least' – *he had been brilliant in his legal career.*
'At least' – *you have two other living children.*
'At least' – *he had lived more than a third of his life expectancy.*

There is **NO** 'at least' when your child dies. I will miss Jono every day of my remaining life and there is no consolation in any of the messages above, so please think carefully before using a phrase starting with *'at least'*.

Other random phrases

As I have previously written, some people have little idea of how impactful their words may be. All I can do is share the comments I did not find helpful around the time of Jono's death. Understanding the power of language may require people to strongly consider what they are about to say to anyone newly bereaved.

'You must not blame yourself.'

Well, if I hadn't thought that before you said it, I sure did after! In psychology this is referred to as the 'pink elephant paradox'. Once someone mentions or suggests something, it then becomes difficult to get it out of your head. The more we try to supress the thought, the bigger and more intense it becomes.

'Oh, another suicide! People tell me "they" prepare for this, and often they are at peace before "it" happens.'
The underlying premise is everyone who dies by suicide follows the 'same' trajectory leading up to death. This is so far from the truth. Every suicide is so very different. The shock and trauma following the suicide of a loved one may have some similarities, but not the actual death.

'Remember to look after yourself' or 'be gentle on yourself' or 'thoughts and prayers are with you and your family'.
All of these sentiments are so well meaning and come from a place of love, but it becomes rhetoric. They certainly are key phrases I used myself in the past without fully appreciating how difficult they are to hear at a time like this.

Self-care immediately following Jono's death was not a priority. Hanging on and breathing was the best I could manage. Sleeping and eating just seemed to happen or not, without much thought or plan. Most actions became automatic.

'Having worked in the area of grief and bereavement will help you at this time.'
The death of Jono felt as though my heart had been ripped out of my body and **nothing** I had learned from my working

experience, or any theories, helped ease that. I was walking brand new terrain. Nothing was familiar to me.

'When you lose a child, the pain is deeper.'
My unsaid response was if I had lost him, I would go and find him. He died. As I mentioned previously, I know we still live in a death denying society and many people don't like using words like 'death', 'died', 'dead', but that is exactly what had just happened. I encourage everyone to please become comfortable using the real words. He has gone from my life because he died.

'How could he do this to his mother?'
He didn't do anything to me. He did it to himself. His pain was so great at that time, I know any thought of me would not have been in his mind. It was his pain, and I was not part of that split second action. From the place he is now, I often imagine that I am sitting with him while he soothes the pain I feel. The day he chose to die, I am almost certain there was no thought given to his family, he just needed to escape his overwhelm.

'No one lives forever—we all have to die somehow.'
All I can say to that is, if that phrase is intended to be helpful, it is not!

'As you work through your grief, the pain will become less.'
Grief is hard. It's bloody hard, but you can't work your way through it. I need to learn to live with my grief and learn

strategies for survival. And I can vouch it is hard work, but I feel different levels of pain every day. Some days are better or worse than others and unfortunately, as I've mentioned before, it does not travel at a linear level. Grief will always live within me, but it will change its shape. An interesting analogy of grief I heard recently described grief like glitter. If you, or children in your life, have ever used glitter, you will know it seems to spread into a million little places. You do your best to clean it up, believing you have swept it all away, but the next week you pick up something, or move something, and there's another huge pile that you hadn't seen when you first cleaned. Sometimes months will go by, and then you suddenly discover a few more sprinkles of glitter that have escaped previous clean ups. Grief is a little like glitter. Sometimes it's big, sometimes it's not so consuming, but you will always find more of it.

'Have you managed to let go of the pain yet?'
Seriously? The pain will never leave me, and it is not something I can 'let go' of. Eventually, I will learn new ways of living with it, but there is nothing to let go of.

'This will help bring closure.'
Like the above, but often referring to a particular event. I recall the police using this phrase about receiving a copy of the police brief that was going to the Coroner's Court. I responded with something like, 'I will never be able to close my thoughts

about my son dying', but one day hopefully, it may not hurt so deeply. Any event or happening, or declaration, will not 'bring closure'.

'Things will change for you as the grief process changes.'
The words 'grief process' (which, by the way, I used to say all the time) now reminds me of the processed meat I might purchase from the deli in the supermarket. In one sense there is no 'process', instead there is the **beginning** the **middle** and **forever**. Oh, it would be so much easier if the 'process' just happened and then one day I felt better, but it is not a mathematical equation to be solved or processed. It simply continues.

All the words that people said to me I am sure were said with good intentions. I graciously accepted them. As I have already said, most often people don't know what to say or what to do and I am not ungrateful for any of the support that was given so freely and lovingly. Some people may misconstrue what I have just written as me being in my 'angry phase' (whatever that is supposed to mean) or even ungrateful. I am neither. I just encourage people to consider their language before providing advice or good intentions.

Even when people offered any of the previous statements, I came to understand they meant no malice. They simply did not put thought into their words. I don't believe their intention was ever to cause more discomfort or hurt, but sometimes it did. It was a reminder for me that perhaps in the past I had also said some of those things. Being on the receiving end, I realised I was on a very steep learning curve.

What I do need to repeat is there were more beautiful, generous supportive souls than those that caused any unintentional upset. It has been said that the strength of humanity is always accentuated in adversity and what my tribe did for me during this time, and continue to do, is beyond words and will always be remembered.

The unannounced visits, usually accompanied with either flowers or food and wine, or all three, were so appreciated. Amidst the pain and despair, I was so frequently reminded of the deep kindness and empathy in this world.

The additional bedding that came into our home to accommodate the extra family members sleeping over just magically appeared.

The texts I received knowing the senders did not expect replies were a gift. They were sent to let me know people were thinking of me and were always comforting.

The simple statement, 'I don't know what to say to you, except you know I love you' was truly welcomed.

From strangers, or professional people that I needed to speak with, their simple 'I'm sorry for your loss' was an acknowledgement that I may be in a tough space and was always so deeply appreciated.

Receiving a box of flowers from my tax accountant four months after Jono died, when I explained why my tax return was late, was truly a melting moment!

When my friends and family hugged me, and gently said, 'Let's cry together', it gave me permission to say nothing at all and just be held. It was very comforting.

Chapter Eleven
Gifts, support and a glimmer of hope

I have written a lot about my pain, and there was and continues to be plenty of it. Along the way, I also managed to identify some activities that have provided *some* softer moments, *some* of the time.

I won't include the most obvious here, such as drink plenty of water, eat healthy food, get plenty of sleep, participate in daily exercise, have yourself some nice hot long baths, and so on. They are all great, and very important, but sometimes the guilt of receiving these suggestions and then realising you have no energy for the basic steps sometimes felt as though I was not trying hard enough to help myself.

I am hoping that if you, or anyone else you may know, has encountered a similar grief experience to mine, that temporary relief might come from considering some of the suggestions listed below. The following activities I speak about gave me some relief but may not be what others choose. I am certainly not endorsing or recommending them, rather just letting you know what has helped me on some days. If you are a recently bereaved parent, you may not have the energy to consider them right now, but perhaps one day in the future some of these ideas might be appealing to you and also offer you comfort.

Acknowledging a mother's grief

It was heart-wrenching to be confronted with the knowledge and truth that there are many other mothers whose children die before them. I know there are fathers too, but the shared and known experience of carrying and birthing your beautiful baby is a unique experience known only to mothers.

For nine months we nurture and grow our babies inside their special warm and protected cave. We are so careful of the food we eat, and what we drink, thinking always of nourishing that tiny human inside. I remember talking to Jono as I carried him within me, playing music to him and slowly stroking his little body before he was born. And from the first time that beautiful baby is breast fed, all the way through to the day they are weaned, which in my case was eighteen months, we consider everything we put in our mouths so we can provide the very best nutrition to our babies.

Our sleep is never the same. We lay awake listening to their breathing and every little gurgle or grunt they make. Mostly, it's the mum who wakes to feed or change their baby. I know things are quite different now, with more of a focus on sharing the role of parenting, but back in the days when I had my young children it was mainly the role of the mum to be on 'night shift'. And mostly we do it without a second thought because our precious packages were worth every bit of broken sleep.

We remember all the nappies that were changed along the way. Truly, this is a labour of love. Although cloth nappies are hardly heard of these days, disposable nappies were never part of my life with my children.

The haunting memory of the first time I dropped my precious one at childcare and the look of betrayal as I walked away has stayed with me. How wonderful it was for both of us when he ran into my arms at the end of my workday.

I remember the first amazing drawing Jono did that looked like a real person. I was convinced he was bound to be a famous artist by the time he reached his teenage years. The beautiful Mother's Day cards I received made from those tiny little fingers, hardly big enough to hold the fat crayons, will remain in my heart forever.

Then there was that moment I dropped him off for his first day of school as his big eyes looked at me, filled with apprehension. I'm sure there is a part in every mum who believes their child is never ready for the big wide world of school.

I recall the day I blossomed with pride as I watched him receive Pupil of the Week award. Suddenly, my small five foot three self felt seven feet tall, and it must have been the dust in my eyes that caused those tears.

This and many other moments make being a mum so very special.

I can only imagine the overwhelming distress that fathers

also experience when their child dies, and I continue to witness the excruciating pain that Tony goes through following Jono's death. However, I still believe it is a different experience than a mother. There is no competition with one being worse than the other, I just believe the experience is different.

Validating that it was okay to feel this almost indescribable pain, because I was a mother whose son had taken his own life, was in a strange way comforting.

Visiting a medium

For most of my life, I have believed that it is possible to communicate with those who are no longer on this earth. I have met some people who have the skills to bring messages to us from the people we love. I have known, and continue to know, many people who refer to themselves as psychics, mediums, or readers. This gift has always intrigued me, and every few years or so I have paid a visit to one of these people to get a sense of which direction my life might be heading. Nearly always, someone, no longer alive, who I have had a close relationship with, will be present during the session and offer me reassurance and encouragement. I have never doubted the messages come from them.

So, five weeks after Jono died, I booked one of these visits. I was still feeling quite shattered, but I was desperate to have some contact with Jono. As I stepped into the room and closed the door, the medium told me a young male had entered the room with me. She continued, saying it was a young, good-looking man and she hoped she didn't upset me, but she believed it was my son, as he was calling me mum. I dissolved into tears, mainly from relief and gratitude, knowing he was there with me. Even though I believed I had previously felt him, I was always uncertain, wondering whether I was imagining it or not. She continued to relay so many messages from Jono, beginning with 'if he could say sorry to me 100 times a day, he would'. I knew then that somehow Jono had been witnessing my trauma and grief. For the next hour, this amazing medium shed light on many things that I had been questioning. Not all of what she said was clear at that time, but as the days and months passed, I remembered what I had been told on that day and it made it easier to understand when I realised later that many more things were coming together.

The experience of feeling so close to Jono shook me to the core and I was a crying mess at the end of the reading. I knew in my mind, however, that my tears weren't caused by trauma but gratitude and a knowledge that he was still around me. During the reading, he promised he would always be there beside me. Whenever I needed him, he reassured me he would be there. All I had to do was ask.

Tree of Souls

I am fortunate enough to live in a very community-minded location, and it didn't take me long to learn about the proposed Tree of Souls. Several beautiful women whose sons had died way before their time (whatever that might be) came together and wondered if there were other mothers who were challenged by the idea of facing Christmas without their children. Symbolically, they wanted to gift something special to their children who had died. One of those mothers had a huge weeping tree in her front garden and offered to display the photos of all of our much-loved children from its limbs. We each submitted our photos which these wonderful women turned into baubles and then laminated them. They displayed all these baubles by hanging them from the 'Tree of Souls'.

Just two nights before Christmas, we all gathered around the tree for a vigil. Meeting other parents whose children's photos were waving in the wind was such an honour and so humbling. The ages of our children ranged from twelve days into their forties. Each of those souls, who were no longer physically on this earth, were being remembered and honoured at this vigil. We lit candles and listened to this beautiful poem written by Tahlia Hunter.[8]

A Love Letter from Those Who Have Passed On
Take the love you have for me and radiate it outwards,
allowing it to touch and impact others.
Take the memory you have of me and use it as a source of
inspiration to live fully, meaningfully and intentionally.
Take the image you have of me in your mind and allow it to fuel
you to take action.
Seize the day and be reminded of what is most important in life.

Take the care you have for me and let it remind you to care for yourself fully and shower yourself with your own love.
And take the pain and grief you feel following my loss and alchemize it into
love, compassion and beauty.
Build a castle from the wreckage of my passing and allow it to unlock your greatness and potential and empower you to become more than you ever thought you were capable of being.
Know that I can never truly leave you and will always remain beside you watching over you in spirit.
Know that the love I have for you lives on through the connections you form, the kindness and compassion you share, and the future relationships and friendships you cultivate.
Until we are one day reunited, I will remain with you through the storms and chaos of life.
I am always beside you, walking with you, laughing with you, crying with you and smiling with you.
I am proud of you for being strong.
I am proud of you for being brave.
And I am proud of you for being you.

The words said it all! Uncannily, my sister had discovered this poem and sent it to me the day before. I was relieved she had, as the words were so evocative it may have totally undone me had I heard it for the first time that night.

Gathering as a group was a significant way of honouring our children, sharing our sadness, and accepting we were all about to experience a similar glaring loss on Christmas Day. That loss united all of us. I have remained in touch with some of these mums, and while it is a group we would all much rather not belong to, it brings much comfort as we support each other. We know we can say anything, and usually do, without needing to explain or apologise.

Online grief community

I was surprised to discover so many grief support groups online. Facebook has so many groups inviting people who may be facing a similar situation to join. They have many benefits, but I think, as a newly bereaved person, one needs to enter any social media community with caution. Unlike attending face-to-face support groups, online membership comes from all over the globe. For me, as I read the sad and distressed posts of many, I was left feeling the weight and despair of so many other people. I soon realised I needed to leave quite a few of those groups because it was not helpful to feel the burden of others while my own pain was still so fresh and raw. In the early days, it was some kind of strange comfort to know that there were other people who had faced a similar trauma. There were always so many members ready to offer words of support and love. I gauged my response as I read some of these posts and realised it was not always positive. When I read posts from someone who may had been bereaved for six years or more, and they still described every single day being filled with pain and hopelessness, it did not give me any hope.

And to the other extreme, there were many in the group who insisted that all one needed to do was to pray and they would feel much better. I totally understand how true this may be for many, but when I read that it felt slightly judgemental. Much like my daily journey of grief, my experience of such Facebook groups fluctuated every day. The question I needed to ask was: do these groups help me in my grief journey or are they harmful? Well, it certainly made me appreciate the real face-to-face support I have in my friends and family, along with my visits to my psychologist. It appeared that many people online did not have the same support as me, and in that situation, it must have been comforting to belong to a group where love and support were accessible. There is no doubt social media has a place in grief, but it may not be for everyone.

In contrast, I also found many pages where beautiful poetry was shared. Lots of the written word I came across provided a soothing massage to my soul. Some amazing people have such a gift with wordcraft and a deep capacity of insight and self-awareness. Sometimes I would wonder, as I read such poetry, whether they had access to my own mind. There were many poems that resonated so strongly with what I was feeling on that day. And yes, that did provide comfort to me in my grief.

The gift of silence

Grief is exhausting and there are days I feel absolutely shattered. There are days when I don't feel like speaking with anyone. There are some days when I just want to hide under a blanket. Even living in a loving relationship, feeling free to do whatever you need in that moment becomes easier if you spend some time on your own.

I am very fortunate to have a close friend who offered her beach house to me for a few days, and I willingly accepted her offer.

About four months after Jono died, I spent five days on my own and in between many beach walks and even a swim in the ocean, I just spent time with me. In one sense, it felt as though I had brought Jono away with me and we were just hanging out with each other. In truth, my heart was searching for Jono everywhere. I was desperately trying to 'be with him'. Perhaps I should clarify that I wanted him to be with me, because during my time away I did not feel as though I wanted to end my life, but I did want him to be beside me in my life.

I welcomed the silence. It is surprising how much we can hear in silence. It is a safe place where we can allow ourselves to be present and just be. Even though I feel enormous suffering, I somehow try to find meaning within this suffering. At times during the grief experience, I am reminded, as I have already said, that we simply need to breathe. It helps us to hang on. And there were times when I continued to sit with my breath—slowly in and holding and slowly out—and tried not to think of anything except my breath.

The second morning at my beach retreat, I awoke at 7:30 am, but as I hadn't slept well I decided to close my eyes and welcomed more sleep. I must have fallen into a deep sleep because the next thing I was aware of was hearing was a deep voice, very Jono-like, simply saying 'hello'. I slowly opened my eyes, uncertain if someone was in the house or not. I looked and there was no one there. Maybe it was just in my dreams, but I like to think it was Jono telling me I should get out of bed and not waste the day!

One day I simply went cloud searching on my long beach walk. I found so many heart-shaped clouds. Big ones, smaller ones, and sometimes all joined together. This was my sign that Jono continued to send his love. I am always searching for ways to bring his spiritual self close to me.

I realised that each person must search for their own meaning. It does not simply come to you without searching. If we want to feel close to something, or someone, we must focus on that and believe what we are experiencing is our truth. Whatever we receive is meant for us alone. For me, all the many signs I continue to receive confirm that Jono and his love are still with me.

Spending that time away from everyone was magical, but I was ready to come back to the welcoming arms of Perry. I learned through this experience that there are likely to be many times when I will need my own space and just 'be' with myself. I know those closest to me understand and support this.

Journaling

I have recommended daily journaling to bereaved people many times. I would often suggest sitting for five minutes with a pen in your hand and write whatever comes to mind. I would encourage writing every day and just observe what flows.

However, what I have found comforting, which started as a brief letter to Jono, soon became daily notes to him. There were things I wanted to tell him about my day, or about what happened during the week, or about the latest sports results, or about the special recipes I had cooked, or about who we had over to share meals with, or about some crazy statement from a politician. These are all the things we used to talk about during our regular phone calls to each other. I miss those calls, so my letter writing was important.

One of my early letters to him was written on the day he would have been due to return from his planned trip to the UK. In my note that day, I imagined I was welcoming him back and told him I was going to be there for him to help him create a new home. I spoke as though he had accepted moving on from any previous stress and I assured him that things would soon become more positive. If only it could have been what I had been able to tell him, had he returned from his trip. In some strange way, I still gained comfort from the things I wrote.

As I look back at the many pages I have written to him, which is now nearly a book full, I notice that almost always I tell him how much I miss him and how much I love him. I continue to tell him that daily. When he was alive, I would always end my phone calls with 'I love you', as he would with me.

Ultimately, writing this book you are reading has proven to be helpful. I'm not sure if it's because I can release the whole story from within me or because I'm passionate about people knowing about Jono and the journey he has sent me on. Most importantly, I want to encourage other parents whose children have died to keep 'holding on' and to remember to take those deep breaths. Even on days when it is difficult, reach out and feel the love of your child who envelopes you from the next dimension. The veil that separates us from our children who are no longer physically here, I am continuing to learn, is ever so thin. Welcome and receive hugs from those close to you who do not need to use words.

Seeking professional support

There are many times in life when people are hesitant to reach out for professional help. If your child dies, you will need support and professional help of some description.

Everyone must find what is right for them, and it will be different for every single human. There are some very helpful and credible phone helplines available (please see the list of resources at the end of this book) if that feels comfortable for you.

There are some great support groups out there too, either online or face-to-face. Some people feel more comfortable being with others who may have had similar experiences.

For me, I felt I needed to sit with someone face-to-face who could reassure me I had the strength to remain here in this world with my pain, pain that I now think will never be completely resolved. If I understand my pain, without it defining who I am, then I feel more able to continue each day. I encourage every bereaved parent to research types of support they feel could be beneficial. As I have already mentioned, I did a search for a psychologist in my location who had expertise in grief. I thought I would benefit from one or two sessions; however, as I write this, I am still meeting with them every five or six weeks. It has been and continues to be incredibly beneficial. I was clear, right at the beginning, that I didn't want anyone telling me how to 'do' grief and pat me on the hand, providing paternalistic platitudes. Despite having been a grief counsellor in the past, nothing I previously thought I knew about grief was making sense anymore. Again, I strongly recommend anyone who might be struggling to make sense of their grief journey to seek a professional of their choice, and my choice was a psychologist. Meeting with them regularly has been an unexpected and amazing support that has helped me to navigate my new world. I can tell them anything, totally unfiltered, and I don't have to worry about upsetting them, or being judged on some of my views or even my language (which can sometimes be colourful!). Their knowledge of the mind is extensive and nothing I say is a surprise to them. The benefits I receive after I have seen them include feeling centred and anchored, and I continually re-establish belief in myself. They validate what I am living with and facing daily. They confirm that my responses are proportionate, which is something I have doubted on many occasions.

Jono's clothing

The day we identified Jono at the Coroner's Court, we made a visit to his house and I was fortunate enough to retrieve some of his clothing. I chose his ties and his socks, for some reason feeling they were important. I also asked for some of his shirts which were familiar clothes I had remembered him wearing. Before I left his room that day, I gathered an armful of unwashed t-shirts from his laundry basket that he had worn when he was exercising, so they still had his special smell. My eldest son later gave me Jono's pillow that he had also brought back that day. There have been many times since that I have buried my head into it and tried to breathe Jono into me. I am forever wondering what was in his mind during the last night he tried to sleep on this pillow. Somehow, I feel comforted by this pillow, knowing it was the last place he laid his head.

As I said previously, most family members wore one of his ties to his funeral as a way of honouring our Jono. I have one or two special ties which I still wear on significant days.

When I wear Jono's socks, which is nearly every day during winter, I feel closely bonded to him. It feels like a well-kept secret. No one else can see or needs to know that I have his socks on my feet, but I feel that bond as I take each step.

I decided that his shirts needed to be kept by us, his

family, but not necessarily for wearing. I proceeded to deconstruct every shirt I had of Jono's. That task alone was very therapeutic. Slowly, very slowly, with my little 'quick-un-pick', stitch by stitch, seam by seam, I collected lots of fabric from each shirt. A friend of mine suggested I just cut them to save time, but that would not have felt right. Each shirt took me quite some time to take apart, as I lovingly laid out the individual pieces before me. I felt such a strong connection with Jono while I was doing this. I even imagined his comments about some special shirts. The one he had worn to his friend's wedding, or about the shop he had bought it from, or the ones I remember being his favourites.

My mission was to complete a small patchwork zipped bag for every member of the family for the first Christmas without him, made from the fabric of his clothes.

Not having ever been a quilter, I did call on some expert advice. Friends were always so willing to help in any way they could, and this was such an interesting new craft to learn. I completed one bag and then other things started to slowly take up my spare time, and so that task was put aside. This is something I do not want to rush, and even though I still haven't quite got there just yet, I know each family member will finally receive a nice little zipped bag made from Jono's clothing. His clothes have been repurposed and will continued to be used, as we continue to have a part of him in our lives.

Tattoo

Even though Jono did not have a tattoo, he had been designing one to get on his UK trip. He had planned to get the Arsenal logo with the two cannons. I have been told that's why they are referred to as the 'gunners'. But he didn't get there and so he died without a tattoo.

I thought long and hard and at age 66, with help from one of Jono's friends, designed my first tattoo. I wanted a fine ink tattoo with the initial of his first name and an image on the inside. I cannot claim to be a Buddhist, however it is a belief system I try to live by. They have a beautiful symbol for transcendence, or love, which I chose to place inside the letter J and there was my tattoo design.

I grew up in a judgemental age where only 'certain types of people' had a tattoo and our family did not even know anyone with a tattoo! Currently, our society appears to be reverting to the very acceptable idea of tattoos simply being ornaments worn on our skin. I carefully researched many tattoo artists until I was happy with the 'all girl' tattoo studio, not far from where I live.

It was around the six-month anniversary of Jono's death when I received my first (and probably only) tattoo on the lower inside of my arm. I just love it and look at it frequently. It is a way of honouring him and is strangely comforting. I'm sure Jono would approve.

Glimmer journal

I had been one of those people who kept a gratitude journal for many years. I started my day noting at least five things I was grateful for and set my intentions for the day. It was a practice that helped me start every day. It probably stemmed from when, as a family, we would sit around the meal table and share at least one good thing that had happened to each of us that day.

After Jono died, trying to imagine I could be grateful for anything seemed almost impossible. All I wanted was for him to be back here, and there was little I could find to be grateful for.

I shared this feeling during a visit to my psychologist who appeared to understand my dilemma and suggested instead, a 'glimmer journal'. Every time I felt a slight glimmer of hope or happiness, I would record it. It felt like small steps, but it helped enormously. I now have a glimmer journal, where I record any small action, or event, or thoughts that occur during the day where I feel some ray of sunshine falling on my life. It doesn't feel as overwhelming as 'gratitude', but neither does it make me feel like someone who is so self-centred they cannot see beyond themselves.

Plants and gardening

Like any activity, people need to find something that brings peace and/or enjoyment. I am blessed to live close to the hills in Melbourne, and we have an abundance of nature walks which provide many opportunities for me to admire local

Chapter Eleven   Gifts, support and a glimmer of hope

native plants and walk amongst the bush.

We are also lucky enough to have a large enough house block which has capacity for lots of garden beds. Alongside the native plants (inspired by my walks), we have several vegetable gardens. Even though I know people who garden should wear gloves all the time, I know when my hands connect directly with the soil something soothing happens. Over the last few years, I have started collecting my own seeds. I am using mini hot houses to grow many plants from seed and then plant them back into the garden. I am not known for my professional gardening prowess, or even for knowing the names of some of the things I grow, but I do know that something special takes place when I am in my garden. As well as feeling a connection with the soil, I somehow also hear Jono's voice. He loved lying in the hammock in our garden with a glass of red, reading a book, and often falling asleep. I know it was his special place to be. So, gardening ticks a few boxes for me, which means I continue to spend a lot of time outside, and always in continual awe of nature and how sunshine and rain help to grow and evolve many wonderful plants and vegetables.

Jono also enjoyed indoor plants and had a couple in his office at work. The day of the gathering at his workplace after he died, when we went to his office, there were two indoor plants which my eldest son and I took home. They have grown and spread beyond belief since being with us. So much so, that we have successfully taken cuttings and produced many more plants from the two that came from his office. We lovingly water and nurture these as an ongoing reminder of the way Jono had done the same.

Opposite handwriting

I remember using this technique when my mother-in-law was dying. I wrote from my heart, detailing exactly how I was feeling about her impending death.

In one of my deeply distressing moments, shortly after Jono died, I chose to try this again.

It goes something like this: create a safe place and take some deep breaths. If you are used to meditating, try to reach a meditative space by relaxing and being aware of your breath. Ask your person who has died what is it they would like you to know right now. Ask if they have a particular message they would like you to know. When you are feeling relaxed, take a pen and paper, and place the pen in the hand opposite to the one you would normally write with, your non-dominant hand.

My letter started with 'Dear Mum', and what followed was a message that felt like it might have come directly from Jono. There is a scientific explanation about using non-dominant handwriting, which helps to draw on creativity. It transcends the boundaries of simple motor skills. Some say it is a great way to access the voice of our inner child, and accessing places that take us beyond our normal rational and linear thoughts. Don't expect lengthy words to flow as it will be basic. Don't expect correct grammar, or possibly even correct spelling. What came to me was raw emotion and I felt I had received a very soothing message from Jono. For me, it worked. It may not for everyone. A lot of people are hesitant because they don't believe they can write with their opposite hand, but believe me, even though it may not look pretty, we can all do it. Remember, you are the only one who needs to read it.

Music

While this might be considered one of those basic suggestions mentioned at the beginning of this chapter, for me it meant not only listening to but making music.

Jono had a very eclectic but strong love of music. I recall when I spent time living in the UK some years ago, excitedly telling him on a phone call back to Australia that I was going to hear a band I had known really well when I was growing up. When he asked their name, my reply was something like 'I'm sure you won't have heard of them. They are called 'The Kinks'.' To my utter surprise, he reeled off some of his favourite songs from this band!

The final Christmas gift I gave him (at his request) was an Arabic record (yes ... a vinyl LP), that was electronic disco mixed with jazz! A very unusual style, but that reflected Jono's tastes.

During my days of darkness following Jono's death, listening to classical music was very soothing. I also have a favourite blues man, Eric Bibb, who seems to write songs that reach into my internal being. Jono would often accuse me of stalking Eric Bibb, as I would go to many of his gigs, both in the UK and Australia, and have had several photos taken standing next to him! Eric Bibb's songs were very comforting for me during those early very dark days.

When Jono's ashes came home, the plain bamboo cylinder sat on top of our piano and they are still there. I am not a great pianist, but I do enjoy playing special pieces to Jono. Some of the older classical pieces, particularly 'Für Elise', Jono heard me playing many times during his growing up years. It is one of my favourite pieces to play and I somehow feel like Jono is listening to me. Making music, by playing any instrument, or using your voice as an instrument, can bring peace and calm, even if just for the moment.

Saying No

Being an extrovert, I have frequently tried to fit many people in my life and attend many social occasions. I used to enjoy people and the social gatherings that once brought such joy. When Jono died, so did my capacity to be around a lot of people. What I would have previously jumped to attend, I found I no longer had the energy or capacity to enjoy. I started saying 'no' to many things. I had always been afraid of offending people if I declined invitations, but now I felt I had no choice. I said 'no' and it helped me to manage each day. I encourage anyone in their mourning journey to make sure they only participate and do what will bring strength and calm. You may feel the most depleted you ever have, as I was in the early days, and there is often nothing left in the tank to give. Sometimes, it is in our best interest to practice saying no.

I hope that as you read all the things that provided calm, peace or strength to me, you are able to consider what it is in your life that may offer the same to you.

Ritual

I have always been a great fan of ritual and have practiced many of them over many decades. I have felt their significance because they supported a particular belief or a certain way I felt. It has helped me to create meaning within my life. As I reflect on my life, I can see that growing up in a family who were regular churchgoers provided a basis for my connection of ritual, although I was unaware of it then. Ritual always speaks directly to my soul.

I now realise that part of my attraction to becoming a celebrant was to do with creating rituals within both weddings and funerals. I find them significant on a grand scale, but also beneficial when completed individually.

Following Jono's death, I felt I had little creative juice left within me. A part of my inside voice kept encouraging me to think of ritual, but my internal tank was empty.

Months later I realised that even though my rituals were not significant, I had been participating in ritual nearly every day.

- I would lovingly put his socks on my feet every day
- I would look at his photo on my wall as soon as I woke up

- I would touch the bamboo urn holding his ashes every day
- I lit a candle on our dinner table every night
- I would write a daily journal entry to Jono.

Rituals do not have to be large or extravagant, what is important is the meaning we give them as we participate in them. It engages our soul. Participating in ritual provides a moment to pause and be mindful of what we are doing. It brings a moment of peace or stillness in a grief-filled day.

Letting people know how you feel

What we do; what we think; what we want; what we don't want, will be so very different and unique for everyone who has experienced the death of their child. I have shared my own experience with the hope it may resonate with others who have lived a similar experience. I also hope that if you are supporting someone who has survived the death of their child, you may have gleaned some helpful insights into ways of supporting and understanding that person by reading this book.

What I have listed below is how I might feel at different times. It will be different for each person, but it is good to remind people around you how it might be for you.

This is how it was for me:
- I might cry a lot
- I might not cry at all
- I might change my mood quickly
- I might want to spend more time on my own

- I might not be clear about decisions I make
- I might not be able to sleep
- I might want to sleep all the time
- I might eat more than I normally do
- I might not eat as much as I used to
- You might think I am frequently confused
- I might experience a shorter than normal attention span
- My memory may not be as good as it was
- I might appear emotionally numb
- I might show more anxiety or fear than normal
- I will probably be much sadder than normal
- I may experience physical symptoms like headaches, nausea, lack of energy, shaking.

I'M OKAY - I'M NOT GOING CRAZY - I'M GRIEVING

If you are supporting someone who is grieving, here are a few practical things that will help.

- Talk about the person who died—use their name in conversation.
- Feel comfortable with words or with silence, crying or not crying.
- Remember special occasions like birthdays or anniversaries.
- Do not judge the bereaved person's behaviour.

- Don't try to hide your own grief if you knew the person who died. If you feel like crying, then cry with your friend.
- Do not use cliches such as, 'You'll get over it one day', 'Just as well you have other children', 'Just think of how lucky you were to have them for so long', 'I know how you feel—my mother died last year'. (Refer back to Ch 10: The power of language.)

I was reminded once that we were born with two ears and one mouth. The significance being that our ears need to work twice as hard as our mouth. So please remember, above all else, the golden rule: be a compassionate listener.

Chapter Twelve
Final thoughts and reflections

As I write this, I have just survived Jono's second anniversary. Some days I reclaim the brighter side of me and feel confident that I can continue with aspects of my life that bring me joy and happiness. Other days, or sometimes even parts of those days, I feel the agonising loss all over again and struggle to get through the next moment.

Someone said to me recently, 'Think of it like you have had your hand severed from your arm. It will heal enough for you to use your arm again, and some days you may be very accepting of it and adjust your life accordingly. On other days you will want to cover it up, and not be reminded of the loss of your hand and wish things were back to how they were before.'

Life will never be like it was before. My grief is a lot like that. I sometimes think I am learning to live without Jono, as a grieving mum who now has a different way of living.

There are many things I have learned from this experience and many more I know I will continue to learn, but something that resonates with me is this: 'Shake hands with grief and welcome her in. She is not the monster you first thought she was. She is love.'[9]

The stronger the love we had for the person who died, the stronger is the pain of our grief.

The following sections consists of words I reflect on from time to time, and while there is nothing amazingly profound about them individually, I am slowly learning the importance of each of them.

Acceptance

I spend a large part of my life reaching for the acceptance that I will never see Jono again. Some days this feels like an impossible task. Other days, when I wear his socks, or talk to his photo, or lay my head on his pillow, I accept that an aspect of him will be with me for the rest of my life.

I now also accept that at the most inopportune moments I may find myself crying. This can be particularly inconvenient if the conversation is with someone I don't know terribly well. Some time ago, I was applying for a credit for some tickets to an event that happened just after Jono died. I thought it would be a straightforward conversation, but there I was, my voice faltering as the tears came and my voice broke up. As in the previous example I gave of my hand being cut off, I need to accept that these moments may continue to happen, and perhaps will for the rest of my life. I am slowly learning to see them not as a weakness of who I am, but the new grieving mother who I am. Some days it can be tough to learn acceptance.

Chapter Twelve   Final thoughts and reflections

Guilt

This incredible emotion has flooded me on many occasions, even when I know it is such a waste of energy. From conception, a mother's priority is focussed on protection. As babies grow into adults, a mother offers the stability of love while at the same time encouraging the independence of their child. Where we can, we always try to protect them from challenging times, or at least stand beside them. Whenever life got tough for Jono he would come to me and we would navigate any challenges together. After Jono made the decision to end his life, I frequently thought I had let him down by not being in the same country when he needed me the most.

I have tried to understand the irrationality of that guilt, especially as it jumps out and bites me from time to time. Can I say emphatically that guilt is an energy that zaps the goodness from all of us. No good ever comes from it. At least I now have the capacity to recognise that and see it for what it is.

Many mothers I have spoken to following their child's death tell me of their sense of guilt. As mothers, we all seem to have the capacity to think of at least one thing we should or should have not done that may have prevented our child dying. Perhaps, in some way, this is also linked to acceptance. We did the best we knew at that time.

Another wise person encouraged me to do the following: to acknowledge and accept all thoughts that come, even the unpleasant ones, but to imagine them as a leaf floating down the stream. You see them, acknowledge them, and then watch them as they disappear down the stream.

There is nothing we could have done to prevent our child's death.

Forgiveness

This act appears to have many edges to it, but I now recognise that with forgiveness comes a certain freedom to one's soul. For me, in relation to the emotion of guilt, I have been able to forgive myself for not being in the same country as Jono when he died. I have been able to forgive myself for not making that one more phone call to him, to check that he was okay. I have been able to forgive myself for not having the capacity to help him change his mind about ending his life.

One day during a reflective time, I realised that any bitterness I may feel towards others and the situation as a whole does not serve me well. When someone takes their life, the circumstances surrounding the last few days of their life is played over and over, as we all try to make sense of it. The first few months after Jono's death, I held on to some very negative thoughts. I tried to imagine situations that he may have found himself in across various aspects of his life. In the absence of not knowing with certainty what took place in those last crucial hours, my imagination was trying to fill the missing gaps.

It takes much less energy not to hold bitterness toward any imagined situation, whether they were perceived as good or bad. To practice forgiveness of anything that may have happened can be calming. Once I had done that, it settled my internal self. I came to accept that I no longer needed to dwell on what I imagined may have taken place.

I made a conscious decision that I would no longer let bitterness impact me. I now sit in a place where there is no bitterness or anger toward anyone or anything. It frees my soul.

Loving kindness

Following on from forgiveness, I can now more fully experience love from others, from myself, and overwhelmingly from Jono.

The kindness that has been demonstrated from family and friends since Jono's death has touched my heart very deeply.

I have already spoken about the padlock of love in our family, which helped us all in those early days. Physically we would stand together with our arms around shoulders, supporting each other. This is how we got through. Even when it was not demonstrated physically, we all knew, from the depths of our souls, that we were in this together. Each of us needed to give and receive the love and the kindness that came with that.

In the very early days, I found it difficult to really identify my needs. One minute I wanted to be totally on my own, while the next minute I felt like being part of a large group. That feeling would change within the same day. Had it not been for the people around me whose love, kindness and understanding were palpable, I may not be here to tell this story. Perry has been my anchor and rock before, during and continuing my grief journey. I will always be thankful to him. I now allow myself to be fully open to receiving all the love that is offered both by Perry and my many other family members and friends.

Before and since Jono died, I have heard so many phrases about love and grief. One that I often see written is that grief is love with nowhere to go. My experience is that love during grief has lots of places to go. As I repeatedly say, I overwhelmingly know that I continue to experience so much love from Jono. I know this is what encourages and motivates me to continue to try to live a purposeful life. What I know is that I still hear Jono in my head every day, with little phrases such as 'well done, Mum', 'you can do this', 'you know I'll be with you', and a lot of other signs and messages that seem to say, 'Keep going. You've got this'.

I have had so many other moments that are sometimes difficult to describe, but I always feel the confirmation that he is with me. From the birds that sing so beautifully when I am sitting outside thinking of him, to the butterfly that came inside, landed on Jono's plant from his office then, ever so gently, just flew back out again. From the many clouds that I see above me in the shape of hearts, to the actual sign on the side of the road that had a huge red heart with one word only: 'Mum'. I sometimes have the sense of someone standing behind me and turn around to find no one there (at least not physically), but I feel the warmth of someone's presence. There are many more examples of the love I feel from Jono and this helps me to spread my love to others. Another phrase I have seen is, 'When we lose someone we love, we must learn not to live without them, but to live with the love they left behind'.

I try to do this every day.

Resilience

I was twelve when my mum died, and it was then I believe I began developing a strong sense of resilience. I left school when I was fifteen and moved from New Zealand to live in Australia when I was sixteen. I was living independently in a shared flat in regional Victoria a few months later. When I returned to New Zealand two years later, I became pregnant and was a single mum at nineteen. Being a single mother in 1975 required much more resilience than today because of societal judgment and pressure. I continued to grow my resilience throughout my life, facing many more adversities, and I believed I was a strong woman. I always tried to see the strengths within my personality. Then Jono died and I no longer felt strong.

There are some days now when that slightly camouflaged and reshaped resilience resurfaces, and I welcome the days I feel strong. There are many other days when it goes back into hiding.

I often ask myself if resilience is something we can learn to develop. If I did not have the baseline resilience I developed at a very young age I am not sure where I would draw any strength from now. The dictionary describes resilience as 'the capacity to withstand or to recover quickly from difficulties'. I know I am a long way from 'recovery' of my grief and it certainly isn't happening quickly, but I have glimmers of hope, confirming that I can hang on. Even though I have been considerably reshaped of late, I will continue, perhaps with a different level of strength. I do not want the death of Jono to define my life as one of absolute misery with me drowning in self-pity. I know he would not want that. I believe he wants me to continue my life in the happiest way possible. It will be a very different kind of happiness than I experienced before, but I will draw from my previous resilient traits to make sure Jono is proud of me.

I often imagine that I have taken this unknown pathway, and I am never sure what lies beyond the next bend. Some of the track is smooth and is such an easy walk, but quite unexpectedly the terrain changes and I suddenly need equipment for some steep rock climbing. During those hard climbs, I know I need to grip tight and just hang on. I need to focus on one foot in front of the other, and so far, I have reached the top of every one of those unexpected cliffs. When I do get to the top, I am often in awe of the view and take deep breaths of recovery. As I continue this pathway, I sometimes find myself on a gentle downward slope and invite others to join me and it becomes a joyous stroll. Then, quite unexpectedly, the terrain changes again, and I am alone in thick forest, being gently caressed by nature. My pathway is never the same for very long. I now feel I have the resilience to at least face the path or journey ahead with the knowledge I will always feel loved and encouraged by others, by Jono, and by myself.

Leaving and creating a legacy

It was obvious at Jono's funeral that the legacy he left was one of great friendship and love for many people. He had made such a difference to the world in his short 31 years and 360 days. He was instrumental in establishing many social groups, and during COVID-19 lockdowns he was the instigator of many creative ways of catching up and connecting with others online or in many other various ways. He was described as the social glue that kept many of his friends together.

Four months after Jono died, we, as a family, participated in a 40 km walk (spread over a month, as I don't think I could have completed it in one walk!) raising money for awareness and prevention of suicide. This was a time that bonded us again and we all felt Jono cheering us on.

He always fought for fair, and his commitment to social justice spurred him on in his career. Not only did he leave a legacy of love for us all, but he also left us a very strong message that we too should continue in his footsteps somehow. Everyone must decide, individually, how they will continue the legacy of their child, depending on individual capacity, availability, and opportunity.

Jono had done many hours of voluntary work for refugees seeking asylum, so I was fortunate on World Refugee Day to be part of the ASRC telethon team. I could feel Jono standing beside me, smiling, as I spoke with many people, accepting each phone donation made that day.

In my celebrancy world I have also made the decision to provide a heavily discounted price to any of his friends or colleagues requesting a ceremony, whether a wedding, naming ceremony or funeral. I will do this in memory of Jono.

I am sure over the coming years there will be more opportunities for future legacies and they will be inspired by Jono.

Beside our home is a laneway that links to the street above us. It has a tunnel of trees and can sometimes feel like a magic pathway. At the beginning of the pathway—next to our driveway—is a grassy patch. I have frequently seen people standing there as they take in the view of the city of Melbourne, or the sunsets, or simply listen to the birdsong. It has always been a special patch. I had a thought I would like a park bench with a plaque to honour Jono, but I had no way of knowing where I could get that situated. I considered the Melbourne Botanic Gardens, or even the parks in the city that Jono would walk through to get to work, but they all seemed beyond reach. One day, we had a local council worker visit us to discuss plans of clearing some overhanging branches. It suddenly occurred to me then, that the most perfect spot for a bench for Jono would be beside our home on the grassy patch.

Chapter Twelve   Final thoughts and reflections

I discussed the idea with the worker, and while he couldn't say whether it was likely to get approval, he suggested I contact the correct department with my request. It did take six months of negotiations, but finally, I was given the fantastic news that the council would proceed with placing the seat where I had suggested. Once installed, they gave me permission to place a plaque in Jono's memory.

The seat was installed and the plaque was ordered. I invited close friends and family to attend a 'Placing of the Plaque' afternoon, followed by drinks and food. I had asked Jono in my mind for a sunny day. What I didn't expect was a very hot 38-degree day! The umbrellas were used to keep the heat off, not the rain. Tony and Jono's brother and one of Jono's best friends drilled the holes for the screws and placed the plaque. Even though my daughter from London couldn't be with us, she had put together a playlist of music that Jono would have loved. We played music during the placing of the plaque and later on too, as we retreated to the cool of our air-conditioned lounge room. This legacy will always remain ours, and as much as Jono used to love coming to visit, I feel like he now has a permanent seat here.

Acknowledging those special dates

Birthdays

In chapter four, I mentioned it was only five days after Jono died that his birthday was upon us. I described how we celebrated that. His birthday the following year still felt like it needed recognition. Every individual will have their own feelings about how they mark their child's birthdays—or not. As a mother, I want to celebrate the wonderful day he was born into this world every year that I am alive. A small family dinner, some chatting around special memories, some good wine, and a few laughs. That's how we did it for his second birthday following his death. We have just now passed his third birthday since his death, and while I still wanted to celebrate, I had a strong desire to be on my own for the day. I drove to a beautiful spot in the Dandenong Ranges with a view of an amazing landscape and watched the video of his funeral. I was reminded how many people would be remembering him on his birthday. I had a coffee in a warm café and wrote a lengthy message to him in his book, then I spent the rest of the day walking or sitting in nature. Perry and I went to dinner that night and toasted Jono. Each year will be different, but his birthday will continue to be significant for me.

How to commemorate the anniversary

Although I have now experienced three anniversaries since Jono died, these dates can be quite tough. It's difficult to describe the lead-up to the date and I'm sure it will be different for everyone. Even within our own family, it is different for each member.

Let me describe how I approached the first anniversary. I found myself trying to relive the days before he died. I wanted to remember every phone call and all the times we caught up before that dreaded date. I had to replace the thought of 'did I miss something?' with 'what a wonderful time we had then' and 'I'm so glad we shared that day or that evening'. It was comforting to know at this time in that last year, he was still alive and with absolutely no idea what was to follow. And just like being on the shore and watching the tide slowly coming in, or preparing for the tsunami, there is nothing that can done to slow or stop that first anniversary day arriving. The day itself was sombre; it was sad; it was reflective.

His workplace invited our family to join them for morning tea, where they were having a 'pause' in their workday. We had visited several times for various reasons since Jono had died, but that day felt like it might be the last time. To see all his work colleagues gathered again was a poignant moment, both comforting and painful at the same time. As someone with oozing empathy, it was reassuring to mix with others who also missed him and it was important for me to know that they were travelling okay. I walked into each small circle of gathered friends and said, 'Hi. Please tell me something about Jono that I don't know.' We shared stories and laughter and tears and some nice food and a cuppa.

As a family, we followed this visit with lunch at a close-by pub. Again, as nice as it was to all be together, it was sombre and sad and comforting, all at the same time.

The next day, a few close friends and part of our family booked some cabins out of town, and we spent the afternoon and evening together. We had lots of photos, lots of stories, lots of food and some good wine. We invited Jono to be with us in spirit. We also looked at the video that was shown at his funeral, remembering the many parts to his life. We lit lots of tealight candles and placed them in shapes of hearts and scattered others around the room. We played some of the music he enjoyed.

The weeks leading up to Jono's second anniversary surprised me. My logical brain tried to tell me that this time would not be as challenging as the first year, after all, I now seemed to be managing the second of each month much more calmly. But from the date that was the last time I had seen Jono physically, until he died, I found myself reliving the significant moments of those days. They were unexpected thoughts, but ones I accepted. There were times when I remembered to practice my deep breathing which was beneficial.

You may remember my mentioning a blues artist who I particularly enjoy—Eric Bibb. Whenever he had come to Australia on previous tours, we would travel to various places in Victoria to hear him. The closest venue to where we lived that he had played at was probably in the city, which was about an hour's drive away. I was absolutely gobsmacked to read of his next intended tour with a venue near to my house! He was performing five minutes away at Burrinja Cultural Centre. Not only was the venue so close, but the date of his performance was the 2nd of June—Jono's second anniversary. A cynic might simply pass it off as coincidence. I held a much stronger view, as I imagined Jono chuckling to himself as he pulled off this little unexpected bonus on this particular day.

The morning of that day was still very painful as the time of his death approached. Just as soon as that time passes, I am again filled with peace. It is over for him. That is not to say my longing for him remains with me, but the pain that he must have been feeling before his death transforms into calmness. As a family, we then enjoyed an amazing Eric Bibb concert in the afternoon and shared dinner together in the evening.

Each anniversary will be different. For anyone who approaches the death of their person, it will be different. It will be different for each person in the same family. What I do know is that date, June 2nd, will happen once every year. I know I will always need to acknowledge it accordingly, in my own way. Other people will choose what they need to do on different occasions, and there is no right or wrong way.

Christmas Day

I have already mentioned our first Christmas Day, and apart from my own personal crisis on that day, I think as a family we did many things that helped bring Jono into the celebration. The most important thing we did was to include his name in our conversation. We will always use his name as a way of affirming his ongoing importance in our lives.

We chose a very happy photo of Jono, placed it on some red cardboard and laminated it, using it as our 'standout' Christmas decoration hanging from the tree. Traditionally, we eat our Christmas meal outside under the trees, so we brought that decoration outside with us and placed it in the centre of the table. He stayed with us throughout the day. Before we began our meal, we toasted Jono, knowing he would have loved the all the food we had prepared. Other people have told me they set a place at the table and have a vacant chair for their person.

The second Christmas without Jono was the opposite. Although my daughter was not coming from the UK, my eldest son and daughter-in-law were going to join us for a quiet but meaningful day together. Three days before Christmas my son caught COVID-19, a day later his wife caught it and on Christmas Eve, Perry had COVID-19. We had not seen my eldest son for at least ten days, so it was quite an amazing coincidence that COVID-19 kept us apart.

I had another wedding booked on New Year's Eve afternoon, so it was essential that I didn't catch COVID-19 from Perry. Apart from delivering food to his room masked up, I tried my hardest to reduce all contact with him. I had Christmas dinner at the table on my own, looking at the Christmas tree with one of the decorations being a photo of Jono, and thinking warm thoughts of the many wonderful and happy Christmases we had all shared over the years. Perhaps it was meant to be a 'gentle' Christmas.

Chapter Twelve Final thoughts and reflections

Something special

Below is an excerpt written by Nick Cave in response to a question asked of him regarding the death of his son.[10] It was not suicide, he fell from a cliff, aged fifteen. Someone asked him how he deals with this death. His response is rather beautiful.

This is how Cave replied:

> *This is a very beautiful question and*
> *I am grateful that you have asked it.*
> *It seems to me, that if we love, we grieve.*
> *That's the deal.*
> *That's the pact.*
> *Grief and love are forever intertwined. Grief is the terrible reminder of the depths of our love and like love, grief is non-negotiable.*
> *There is a vastness to grief that overwhelms our minuscule selves. We are tiny, trembling clusters of atoms subsumed within grief's awesome presence.*
> *It occupies the core of our being and extends through our fingers to the limits of the universe.*
> *Within that whirling gyre all manner of madness's exists; ghosts and spirits and dream visitations, and everything else that we, in our anguish, will into existence.*
> *These are the precious gifts that are as valid and as real as we need them to be.*
> *They are the spirit guides that lead us out of the darkness.*
> *I feel the presence of my son, all around, but he may not be*

there, I hear him talk to me, parent me, guide me,
though he may not be there.
He visits Susie in her sleep regularly, speaks to her, comforts her,
but he may not be there.
Dread grief trails bright phantoms in its wake.
These spirits are ideas, essentially.
They are our stunned imaginations reawakening after the calamity.
Like ideas, these spirits speak of possibility.
Follow your ideas, because on the other side the idea is change
and growth and redemption. Create your spirits.
Call to them.
Will them alive.
Speak to them.
It is their impossible and ghostly hands that draw us back to the
world from which we were jettisoned;
Better now and unimaginably changed.
WITH LOVE, NICK.

These words resonate with me so much. We (grieving parents) certainly are NOT all in the same boat, but from time to time I believe we all experience the effects of the same storm. Acknowledging that there will be storms, despite how our child died, and accepting that for every one of us it will be felt different, may help. What we all have is the power to enhance our connection. As Nick Cave suggests, 'Call to them ... will them [their spirit] alive ... speak to them.'

Chapter Twelve   Final thoughts and reflections

FACING THE UNFATHOMABLE ... surviving your son's suicide—even when you doubt you will.

Support

Because responses to grief are so individual, I will include a breadth of resources that may be helpful. Some have phone numbers while others require searching the web. Please note, the resources provided are for Australia.

If you need help urgently, phone 000.

Suicide Call Back Service: 1300 659 467
Lifeline: 13 11 14
Beyond Blue: 1300 224 636
Headspace: 1800 650 890
Griefline: 1300 845 745
13YARN Aboriginal & Torres Strait Islander crisis support line: 13 92 76
Just one reason: https://justonereason.com.au
Grief Australia: 03 9265 2100 / https://www.grief.org.au/
ReachOut: au.reachout.com
Conversations Matter: https://conversationsmatter.org.au/
Postvention Australia: 1300 024 357 / https://postventionaustralia.org/
Compassionate Friends: 03 9888 4034 / www.compassionatefriendsvictoria.org.au

Head to Health: https://www.headtohealth.gov.au/
StandBy: 1300 727 247 / https://standbysupport.com.au/
Forever Held Foundation: https://foreverheld.org.au/

A selection of resources

We all take what we need when we read, so I wanted to share a list of what helped me. Hopefully, some of these resources will hit the right spot for you.

The first two books listed are written by parents whose child/ren have died. We all approach grief individually, but I found them easy to relate to.

T. Zuba (2014) *Permission to Mourn: A new way to do grief.*

L. Hone (2023) *Resilient Grieving: How to find your way through devastating loss.*

The following books cover general grief.

M. Devine (2017) *It's OK that you're not OK: Meeting Grief and Loss in a Culture That Doesn't Understand.*

J. Kick (2021) *Weathering The Grief Storm: Learning to thrive within loss.*

M. Anthony (2021) *The Afterlife Frequency: The Scientific Proof of Spiritual Contact and How That Awareness Will Change Your Life.*

A. Kagon (2013) *The Afterlife of Billy Fingers: How my bad-boy brother proved to me there's life after death.*

F. Weller (2015) *The Wild Edge of Sorrow: Rituals of Renewal and the Sacred Work of Grief.*

G. A. Bonanno (2019) *The Other Side of Sadness: What the New Science of Bereavement Tells Us About Life After Loss.*

P. Coleman (2014) *Finding Peace When Your Heart Is In Pieces: A Step-by Step Guide to the Other Side of Grief, Loss and Pain.*

The next one is more of an activity book. I used this when I was providing grief counselling.

E. Hodge (1998) *Write Through Loss and Grief: A guide to recovery through writing.*

The following two are more poetry style writing, which I found quite soothing.

D. Ashworth (2022) *Loss: Poems to Better Weather the Many Waves of Grief.*

J. O'Donohue (2007) *Benedictus: A book of Blessings.*

And finally, a textbook that I have always found useful. If you would like a resource with more scientific research, you will find this helpful.

J. Winchester Nadeau (1998) *Families Making Sense of Death.*

Interestingly, Jono borrowed this book from my library the year before his death, when his best friend died. He wanted to be sure he didn't cause harm in his approach to comforting his friend's family.

References

1. Australian Institute of Health and Welfare (2024) *Suicide and self-harm monitoring data*: https://www.aihw.gov.au/suicide-self-harm-monitoring/data/suicide-self-harm-monitoring-data

2. M. Stroebe, H. Schut (1999) *The dual process model of coping with bereavement: rationale and description*, Death Studies, 23:3, 197-224, DOI: 10.1080/074811899201046. https://doi.org/10.1080/074811899201046

3. T. Attig (2001) *Relearning the world: Making and finding meanings.* In R. A. Neimeyer (Ed.), *Meaning reconstruction & the experience of loss* (pp. 33–53). American Psychological Association. https://doi.org/10.1037/10397-002

4. D. Klass, P. R. Silverman, S. Nickman, Eds (1996) *Continuing Bonds: New Understandings of Grief*

5. J. Tremi, K. Linde, E. Brahler and A. Kersting (2024) *Prolonged grief disorder in ICD-11 and DSM-5-TR: differences in prevalence and diagnostic criteria.* Front. Psychiatry 15:1266132. doi: 10.3389/fpsyt2024.1266132

6. S. Beaton, P. Forster, M. Maple: *Suicide and language: Why we shouldn't use the "C" word.* InPsych. 2013; 35(1): 30–3

7. S. Pridmore, J. Ahmadi, W. Pridmore (2019). *Two Mistaken Beliefs about Suicide.* Iranian Journal of Psychiatry,14 (2),182-183. https://www.ncbi.nlm.nih.gov/pmc/articles/PMC6702281/

8. Tahlia Hunter: *A Love Letter from Those Who Have Passed On.* Writer on FaceBook. Used with permission.

9. Donna Ashworth (2023) *Wild Hope: Healing Words to Find Light on Dark Days.* Used with permission.

10. Nick Cave's *Letter to Cynthia,* theredhandfiles.com. Used with permission.

Acknowledgements

There are many people who contribute to a book being written, and I would like to acknowledge some of the people who supported and helped me complete this story.

Firstly, Perry and my family, both immediate and extended, who have supported me in ways beyond description. They were always there for me, even when I didn't know I needed them! They gave me reason to keep going both with living and with writing this book.

My friendship circle is far too wide to thank everyone who has encouraged me in the telling of my story, but if you are reading this, you will know who you are.

My very long-standing friend of more than 40 years, Anice, who gave so generously in my hour of need. The food, the toys for my granddaughters when they arrived in Australia for Jono's funeral, and the messages of hope and love. We have both stood in the same space, and both miss our children who are no longer on this earth.

My friend Sue, who tirelessly read through my manuscript with much encouragement and hours of loving work for the first edit. You really are my soul sister.

My newly found friend Lynne, also known as my book

buddy. What you gave me while I was writing this story is more than words can ever say. You helped connect me to Jono in ways I did not think possible. We stood beside each other, encouraging each other to keep going with both manuscripts.

To all the mums I continue to meet under the banner of 'Tree of Souls'. We carry each other's pain when it is needed, knowing how to laugh and cry in the same sentence. I appreciate your words and company greatly. Thanks Rineke for your vision.

To my very dear friends Carol and Mary Ann who have been beside me in my journey all the way. Thanks for being there.

To my editor, Rebecca Wylie from Sage Written Word, who offered so much more than wise words. Who knew we were to meet on that morning?

To Dr. Peter A. J. Fanning (*BCom, GradDipPsych, BSc(Hons), DPsych(ClinNeuro), MAPS, MCCN*) Registered Psychologist / Clinical Neuropsychologist; who I trusted with my everything. Thank you for showing up in my search.

To all of Jono's friends and colleagues who supported me simply by being there and reminding me how important Jono was to all of you.

And finally, to Jono, for all those little messages I received from you during the writing of this story. You made me so very proud; now, I will try to make you proud.

About The Author

Christine Pedley was born in New Zealand but has lived in Melbourne, Australia, permanently since 1976. She wanted to be an early childhood teacher when she was at school, but after many years figuring out what she was passionate about she became a social worker. She worked initially in the family violence field, later transitioning to palliative care. She is now a wedding/funeral celebrant and a death doula. Her passion was to increase death literacy within the community through workshops and community speaking.

Christine lives at the foot of the Dandenong Ranges with her much loved partner, Perry. She loves to spend time in her garden with the many birds who also call it home.

Her life was turned upside down and inside out when her youngest son unexpectedly took his own life in 2022. Purpose and direction was difficult in the hard times that followed, but Christine is journeying towards an exciting future that focuses on supporting and mentoring those reaching out for more information about death, dying and bereavement. She is an advocate for building compassionate support systems for those who are grieving.

Facing the Unfathomable is Christine's first book. It was written in the hope that it reaches those who are facing similar experiences.

Visit Christine at **www.pedleywrites.au** for more. Subscribe to her newsletter to keep up-to-date with future releases. If this book spoke to you, please consider leaving a review with your retailer. Your voice can help another reader determine if this book is for them too.

www.ingramcontent.com/pod-product-compliance
Lightning Source LLC
Chambersburg PA
CBHW060605080526
44585CB00013B/683